Antonio Vivaldi
and the Baroque Tradition

Antonio Vivaldi
and the Baroque Tradition

Donna Getzinger
Daniel Felsenfeld

MORGAN
REYNOLDS
Publishing, Inc.

620 South Elm Street, Suite 223
Greensboro, North Carolina   27406
http://www.morganreynolds.com

Classical Composers

Johann Sebastian Bach

Antonio Vivaldi

Richard Wagner

Johannes Brahms

George Frideric Handel

ANTONIO VIVALDI AND THE BAROQUE TRADITION

Library of Congress Cataloging-in-Publication Data

Getzinger, Donna.
    Antonio Vivaldi and the Baroque tradition / Donna Getzinger and Daniel
    Felsenfeld.— 1st ed.
       v. cm. — (Classical composers)
    Includes bibliographical references (p.   ) and index.
    Contents: One voice of the Baroque — Music and the priesthood — Operas
    and concertos — The music business — Rumors — Outside of Venice —
    Out of fashion — Vivaldi remembered.
      ISBN 1-931798-20-6 (library binding)
    1. Vivaldi, Antonio, 1678-1741—Juvenile literature. 2.
    Composers—Italy—Biography—Juvenile literature. [1. Vivaldi, Antonio,
    1678-1741. 2. Composers.] I. Felsenfeld, Daniel. II. Title. III.
    Series.
      ML3930.V58G47 2004
      780'.92—dc22

2003019830

To Caylin—
Born to be a new fan
of classical music

Contents

Antonio Vivaldi.

(Engraving by Lambert the Younger.)

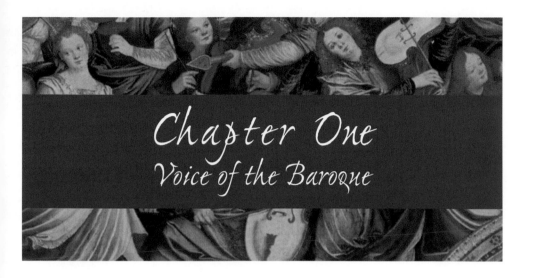

Chapter One
Voice of the Baroque

When Antonio Vivaldi raised his hands, he brought the music to a close on his final concert. On December 19, 1739, his professional career ended where it had begun—conducting the orchestra of a girls' orphanage, the *Pio Ospedale della Pietà*, as they played one of the pieces he had composed for them. Vivaldi had taught at the orphanage to great renown for thirty-six years, but he left his final concert a poor, friendless man, on his way to a self-imposed exile. One of the great composers of the Baroque era, Antonio Vivaldi, sixty-two years old and nearly penniless, was forced to leave the land of his birth for Vienna, in hopes of finding work.

Vivaldi had demonstrated musical talent from a tender age. During the arc of his career he gained tremendous wealth and fame, performing and composing music

1636 view of Venice. Built on a lagoon, Venice is the city of Vivaldi's birth.

for every degree of royalty and noble personage. But less than a week after his final concert, Vivaldi packed his belongings and hired a carriage with what little money he had to spare. The Venice of his younger days— a shining place full of music, spectacle, and opportunity for a poor, sickly barber's son—had changed too much. Vivaldi was unable to change with it. He would never return to Italy.

The circumstances that combined to bring Vivaldi to this low point were both personal and historical. In the

(By Oduardo Fialetti. Courtesy of Eton College, Berkshire.)

1680s, the Italy of Antonio Vivaldi's childhood was divided into separate states, each with its own ruling government and laws. Venice was a republic with an elected senate and leader, called the *Doge,* who was elected for life; powerful merchants controlled the senate. Located in a lagoon in northern Italy, Venice's famed canals serve as reminders of the role the city played as a stopping point on the trade routes between Europe and China. Venetian merchants had been among the wealthiest in Europe during the Renaissance. The canal-lined byways were filled with gambling halls, coffeehouses, brothels, and theaters. Yearly masquerade festivals drew hordes of people, rich and poor, in search of a good time. Glassmaking, printing, and other industries kept the city swimming in money.

From the workshops of the violin makers to the grand opera theaters, music could be heard everywhere. It was part of every religious activity, every child's education, and every adult's entertainment. The nobility built their homes around grand parlors where chamber music concerts were performed. Gondoliers used a single oar to push their boats, called gondolas, up and down the shallow canals, while serenading their passengers. The better they sang, the more money they earned. Rare was the Venetian who did not know how to play an instrument, and rarer still was the shop or business that did not have a few instruments handy for its customers to play while waiting for service.

In the decade of the 1680s, in the heart of this musical city, a crowd of men came nearly every day to visit Giovanni Battista Vivaldi's barbershop. Squeezing themselves into the packed waiting room, their wide-brimmed beaver hats and scratchy wigs came off and they tossed their heavy *justacorps* coats, that were tight at the waist and long enough to cover their puffy breech pants, in a corner to free their arms. Lace cravats around necks were loosened and booted toes tapped the wooden floor. These visitors were not seeking a haircut or shave. They came to listen as the little copper-haired boy in the

Opposite: A gondolier ferries his masked passenger through the Venice canals. Masks were commonly worn during Carnival. *(Detail of a painting by Canaletto, courtesy of the Royal Collection.)*

The Venice of Vivaldi's childhood was a city overflowing with music. *(Courtesy of the National Portrait Gallery, London.)*

middle of the room sawed away at the strings of his battered violin. The boy was Giovanni's oldest son, Antonio Lucio Vivaldi.

Antonio had been born prematurely on March 4, 1678. Since birth, he had suffered from an illness that made him weak and short of breath whenever he exerted himself. Historians now believe he may have had either asthma or angina, a sometimes painful condition in which the heart does not receive enough oxygen. While his younger brothers, Bonaventura and Francesco, ran about town getting into tussles with friends or playing *Pallone,* a game similar to soccer, Antonio had to remain indoors. Isolated from the other children of the busy Italian neighborhood, Antonio filled the long, lonely hours by learning to play music.

Though he usually played at home, his favorite place to practice was at his father's barbershop, where he could take turns trying out any of the various musical instruments. His father responded enthusiastically to his interest in music and often stole moments away from clients to give Antonio lessons on the violin. Luck was with the customer who arrived in time to hear father and son playing together. Giovanni was an excellent violinist, and he knew all the pieces by Arcangelo Corelli and Giuseppe Torelli, famous composers of the era.

Giovanni kept several woodwinds, such as the oboe and bassoon, and a couple of horns on hand, but mainly customers were attracted to his large collection of the *viol* family of stringed instruments. These ranged from the small lute to the hefty cello. The newest and most favored was the violin, which had undergone many changes since its invention in the sixteenth century. The instrument had become both flatter and rounder, and the size of the sound holes were modified from a c-shape to an f-shape. Earlier models had been rested on the knee while played but by Vivaldi's time violins were rested on the shoulder. (Today violins rest under the chin.) The best violins in Italy were crafted by Niccolò Amati and his former student Antonio Stradivari. Amati was a

Gaspar Duiffoprugcar, pictured in this engraving from 1562, belonged to a family famous for their instrument making. He lived in Lyons, France.

member of a legendary Italian violin-making family; his grandfather Andrea is credited with the basic design of the modern violin. When the bow made of horsehair slid across the strings made of cat intestine, a rich and lively sound came from the instrument. In the hands of players such as young Antonio or his father, the violin brought forth smiles, tears, or sighs of melancholy delight from listeners.

Antonio's father worked as a barber and also in the

Two of Stradivari's intricately detailed designs for the scroll of the violin.

family bakery until 1685, when he became a professional musician. He was twenty-nine years old. As a
soloist in the orchestra of *Basilica San Marco* (St. Mark's
Chapel), the elder Vivaldi played for the renowned conductor Giovanni Legrenzi. The St. Mark's orchestra had
been in existence for hundreds of years, and every
conductor, or *maestro di cappella,* in the group's history
had been a musician revered throughout Italy. Giovanni
Vivaldi was a featured performer and earned more money
than any of the other players. The public loved to give
nicknames to their favorite artists and had dubbed
Giovanni "Baptista Rossi." *Rossi* means "red" in Italian

and referred to Giovanni's head of bright red hair.

Giovanni tried to teach music to his other sons and his three daughters, Margherita, Cecilia and Zanetta. The boys did not show much interest, and the girls were too busy tending to chores, such as shopping, cooking, and washing clothes. Laundry itself was a huge task that could easily occupy several days of the week. Men and women wore many layers of clothing, which included stockings, blouses, fanciful bows and ribbons, vests, coats, capes, petticoats, puffy short pants, and high-heeled shoes. The excessive detail in the fashions exemplifies how beauty and extravagance dominated every aspect of Venetian culture.

With the rest of the family busy with other activities, young Antonio was the only child who took advantage of the extra attention he got from his father when he appeared at the barbershop for his afternoon lessons. Antonio knew he had pleased Giovanni when he pulled his prized Stradivarius violin off the top shelf and let Antonio play it after the shop closed. Nobody else was allowed to touch it.

In 1689, Giovanni introduced ten-year-old Antonio to the great Legrenzi at St. Mark's Chapel. Antonio played the violin for Legrenzi and impressed the famous conductor so much that Legrenzi invited Antonio to substitute in the orchestra whenever Giovanni was unavailable. Not only was this opportunity a great honor, it made him the youngest member of the St. Mark's orchestra.

The musician's gallery at St. Mark's Chapel, in a drawing by Venetian painter Canaletto. *(Courtesy of Kunsthalle, Hamburg.)*

Antonio Vivaldi was entering the world of music at an auspicious time. Born in the middle of what would come to be called the Baroque period, Antonio was surrounded by music characterized by an elaborate and ornamental style. New instruments were being developed or refined, among them the clarinet, the flute, and the oboe. Improvements were being made to the major stringed instruments, and the very way music was played was evolving from the styles that had prevailed in earlier periods.

The Middle Ages (1200-1450) had produced music in two broad categories: sacred and secular. Sacred music had to do with religious ceremonies and usually consisted of one or two voices chanting. Secular music was music outside of the church, and it too was very simple. Both kinds of music used very little instrumen-

A group of musical entertainers from the Middle Ages, playing cymbals, a harp, and a lute-like instrument. *(Courtesy of Scala/Art Resource, New York.)*

Roman ruins, depicted here in the 1680s by Viviano Codazzi. During the Renaissance, artists, scientists, and scholars returned to the art, achitecture, and literature of ancient Greece and Rome. *(Galleria dell'Academia di S. Luca, Rome.)*

tation, and the idea of harmony (several voices singing together at different pitches) was just beginning to be explored.

During the Renaissance (1450-1600), the artistic and literary traditions of ancient Greece and Rome were rediscovered, which led to great shifts in science and the arts. Changes in political and religious structures meant people were freer to consider ideas and possibilities outside of the Church. Inspired by these long-forgotten cultures, the people of the Renaissance infused their art, literature, science, and architecture with a renewed sense of vigor. Music became more complex and ornate, beginning a trend that continued through Vivaldi's career.

The music Vivaldi composed is characterized by a

richly textured sound. He wrote multiple melodies to be played simultaneously, a technique that added warmth and density to the music. Vivaldi's violins, his favorite instrument, are given the freedom to fly over the rest of the orchestra. Rhythmically exuberant fast movements balance his slow passages, which are typically full of long, gentle notes entwined to give the sense of sorrow or mystery. Vivaldi's work on the concerto revolutionized the form.

Although Baroque music was highly sophisticated and technical, musical notation (the act of representing sounds on the page) was not yet a totally polished system. The technique was, however, advanced enough to make composing music a legitimate occupation, where previously music had been passed along

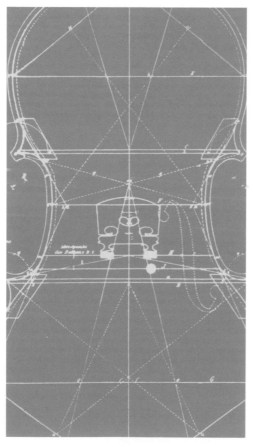

Antonio Vivaldi was passionate about the violin from an early age. Later, his compositions would feature brilliant violin solos.

primarily by ear. Now, composers communicated the various sounds they wanted each instrument to make through a standardized system of symbols. This ability to capture and convey sounds more precisely put a new emphasis on the form of the music itself. Composers became concerned with complex patterns and rigorous structures and, some would argue, it was not until the Classical period (beginning about 1750) that composers tore themselves away from this fascination with form and became more concerned with content.

This is not to say that the music Antonio Vivaldi heard and played as a child was mathematical and overly complicated. It was beautifully ornate and greatly respected in Europe. Indeed, the music of Venice brought laughter, love, sadness, hope, and even despair to its listeners. Talented Venetian musicians enthralled the western world and were awarded superstar status. The best of them were employed to write and perform for the royal courts of Europe.

By 1691, twelve-year-old Antonio had written his first piece of music—a vocal work for the Church called *Laetatus*. Antonio's early flirtation with composing was a brief one, however. His first passion was the violin. Playing with his father and the orchestra at St. Mark's helped Antonio hone his talent. More than merely father and son, Antonio and Giovanni became partners. For three years this father-son team, with their matching heads of fiery red hair, played violin duets together at local theaters and church festivals. The elder Vivaldi had

composed a few of these duets, but most of their repertoire featured works by popular composers of the era.

Antonio was always experimenting with the range of
notes on the violin and the speed at which he could play
them. He wanted to be the best violinist in Italy. His wild
playing style became his signature—fingers fluttering
at lightning speed over the fingerboard, playing pitches
higher than any other violinist had ever been able to
achieve. To accommodate his flamboyant playing style,
Antonio even had a special violin crafted. His violin had
an especially long neck, so that he could reach even
higher notes than before.

Audiences were astonished and thrilled by his virtuosity whenever Antonio took the lead on his violin. After
hearing Antonio play, Johann Fredrich Armand von
Uffenbach, a German traveler and great lover of music,
wrote, "…it is hardly possible that anyone has ever
played, or ever will play, in such a fashion. He put his
fingers but a hair's breadth from the bridge, so that there
was scarcely room for the bow, and he did this on all four
strings with fugues and with incredible speed. Everyone
was astounded."

Despite his immense musical talent, as the oldest son
of a family with limited means, Antonio was expected
to enter the priesthood. Younger sons could become
apprentices in a trade or business, but the oldest sons
were expected to be educated. The education that boys
received by entering the clergy was free and led to
respect for the family and a steady income.

Religion was a key element of Italian life. The Catholic Church educated Vivaldi in exchange for his becoming a priest. Above, Catholic priests heal a possessed man while gondoliers maneuver the crowded canals. *(Courtesy of Academia, Venice.)*

Religion in Italy at the time was controlled by the Catholic Church, which was centered in the Vatican, in Rome. The Church was also the most powerful political institution, which over the centuries had been involved in occasional conflicts with the Venetian Republic. By the late seventeenth century, the Church was making an effort to enlist greater numbers of priests, offering families without much money, such as the Vivaldis, an opportunity for social advancement.

When he turned fifteen, Antonio reluctantly quit the concert circuit to prepare for the priesthood. Antonio did not begrudge his father's insistence that he become a priest. After years of playing with the St. Mark's orchestra, working for the Church seemed a natural fit. Besides that, he saw a way that he could both receive an education and continue his musical career. Antonio agreed to pursue the priesthood on one condition—that he not be forced to study in the seminary, a school for boys entering the clergy. He wanted to study privately so he could continue his musical training. Another reason he wanted to study outside the seminary was his lingering poor health. He knew he would receive better attention and care from his mother and sisters than from the priests at school.

Antonio was hardly the first young man to combine an interest in music with a career in the clergy. Talented musicians and composers were encouraged to enter the clergy and use their talents for the betterment of the church. Many priests were also composers, and Pope Clement IX, considered the most amiable of the popes, had at one time written for the opera. The Church had a long history of taking care of musicians. Since Antonio had already shown great prowess as a violinist and some potential as a composer, rules were easily bent in order to keep him interested in pursuing a religious career.

The Church's drive to increase the number of priests also made it easier for Vivaldi to study for the priesthood without studying at a seminary. He was appointed as a priest's assistant, and then studied at two local parishes, San Giovanni in Oleo and San Geminiani, while living at home. His teachers allowed him plenty of opportunity to work at his craft. Along with his academics, he diligently practiced his violin and continued to learn more about composition.

For seven years, September 1693 to September 1700, Antonio moved through school, getting promoted to a new order each autumn. From the age of twenty-one to twenty-four, Antonio took a break from his education to play more concerts with his father. Although it is not certain that he did, he may even have taken time to travel to Rome to study music with Arcangelo Corelli, music master to Cardinal Ottboni. Corelli was considered to be the most accomplished violinist of his time. He was known for the purity of his tone and for his con-

Arcangelo Corelli.

tributions to the growing field of violin technique.

Studying with Corelli would have given Vivaldi a chance to gain more familiarity with the concerto form of music, as Corelli had perfected what is now known as the *concerto grossi*. In this form of music, a *concertino* (a small ensemble group of two to five instruments) played in a call-and-response motif with the larger orchestra. Corelli's concertos had become quite popular, and audiences were clamoring to hear more of them, as well as concertos written by other composers who could capture the same sound.

In later years, Vivialdi's music showed signs of being influenced by Corelli. As he had challenged himself at the violin in his youth, he began to challenge himself in composition. Eventually he forged a compositional style all his own. It would not take long before the term concerto became synonymous more with the name Vivaldi than Corelli.

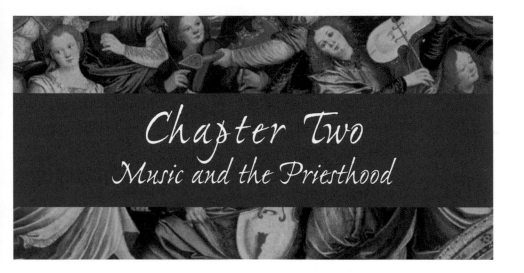

Chapter Two
Music and the Priesthood

Antonio Vivaldi became a priest, on his own terms, in 1703. He was twenty-five years old. Now he needed an assignment that would pay well and allow him to continue working in music. He knew the Church would make use of his musical abilities somehow, but he did not want to merely conduct the choir at a tiny chapel somewhere out in the countryside. He wanted a position that allowed him to stay in the bustling city of Venice, where he could win fame despite having to wear priestly robes. Catholics from every corner of the known world came to Venice, worshipped in the Venetian churches, and heard the music of the Venetian Catholic Masses. The men who composed and conducted that music were highly revered.

Vivaldi would get his wish. Soon after completing his

schooling, Francesco Gasparini, the current *maestro di coro* (musical director) of an all-girls' orphanage in Venice, offered twenty-five year old Vivaldi the position of *maestro di violino* (violin teacher). Vivaldi accepted the post without hesitation, fully aware of the honor of being given this appointment.

This orphanage was no ordinary school. The *Pio Ospedale della Pietà* (The Hospital of Pity and Compassion) had existed for hundreds of years. Located at the edge of the Riva degli Schiavoni, the opening of the Grand Canal into the lagoon that surrounds Venice, the convent school had been built during the Middle Ages to help the unwanted or orphaned babies of the growing Italian population. Three similar institutions existed in Venice, each with a slightly different purpose. The *Derelitti* was a temporary home for desperately impoverished adults and children who needed a place to stay while they searched for work and a permanent place to

Venice's Grand Canal, by Francesco Guardi. *(Courtesy of École des Beaux Arts, Paris.)*

live. The *Incurabli* was a hospital for the incurably sick who needed a place to live out their lives. Orphaned girls who could be taught ended up at the Pietà (orphaned boys were usually taken in by families or businesses).

A child placed in a basket outside the Pietà would be brought in and cared for until adulthood. There, she would get a practical education and, if she showed aptitude, might learn how to play a musical instrument or two. Eventually, to pay for the care and training of these girls, the clergy started having the young ladies perform public concerts for which they charged admission. Over time, the musical reputation of the girls at the Pietà became known throughout Europe, and the school was able to hire some of the most prominent musicians in Italy to teach there.

Some middle- and upper-class Venetians, envious of the musical skills these girls were learning, would send their children to the Pietà even though they were not orphans. The parents would pretend that they had come into some financial trouble or had suffered a disaster, any excuse to get their daughters inside the doors and enrolled for study. Finally, to put an end to this practice, a warning was engraved into the wall that reads:

> May the Lord God strike with curses and excommunications all those who send, or permit their sons and daughters —whether legitimate or natural— to be sent to this Hospital of the Pietà, having the means and ability to bring them up, for they will be obliged to pay back every expense and amount spent on them...

Vivaldi taught for many years at the Pio Ospedale della Pietà. Pictured above, it is the reddish building to the left of the bridge.

The offer of a teaching job at the Pietà reflected Vivaldi's considerable skills as a musician. The position also enabled him to try his hand at composing. Beyond teaching the girls to play violin, he was to write two concertos each month for the girls to perform.

Vivaldi's childhood surrounded by instruments at his father's barbershop now proved especially useful. He had to compose pieces for all the instruments of the orchestra—not just the violin. He refreshed his skills on the bass, viola, cello, and a variety of woodwind instruments. He also schooled himself in the basics of harp-sichord and organ, two instruments that were usually the strongest voices in sacred Baroque music.

It is important to note that what was meant by "orchestra" in the early 1700s is not the same as what is meant by the term today. In the Baroque period an orchestra was relatively small and was not divided into sections. For instance, rather than rows of violins, there might be only one or two violins. Orchestras in smaller towns were comprised of whatever instruments local musicians knew how to play. Sometimes a few musicians knew how to play several instruments, which meant works for that orchestra had to be written so a musician would have time to put one instrument down and pick up another. Fortunately for Vivaldi, his experience had always been with larger, more impressive orchestras such as that at St. Mark's chapel and now the Pietà. At

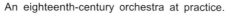

An eighteenth-century orchestra at practice.

the Pietà, enough money was available to provide a large and complete orchestra.

Since he was a teacher, many of the pieces Vivaldi wrote for the girls were simple exercises to improve skills. But the concertos designed for performances were written for advanced musicians. He always wrote to the best of his ability, and he demanded a high level of excellence from his students, though not one of them was over twenty years old. Vivaldi's musical scores often have handwritten notes that reflect the intensity of his style. He had to teach the girls how to hold the bow to achieve precisely the effect he desired; as well, he introduced other violin techniques uniquely his.

The girls performed from a balcony set behind iron screens to keep the audience from being able to see them clearly. Not being able to cast their eyes upon the young performers, the audience could only imagine what they looked like. The screens served two purposes. They provided modesty so the music remained more important than who was performing, and they gave the girls an air of mystery. The music emanating from behind the screens was beautiful enough to convince most audiences that the musicians must be as lovely as angels.

In reality, many of the girls had suffered childhood illnesses or terrible accidents that left them scarred or disfigured. One witness to the backstage life of the Pietà commented in his journals, "Scarcely one was without some considerable blemish. Two or three, however, looked tolerable; they sang only in the choruses." But, when considering their exquisite talent and grace, he added, "Ugliness does not exclude charms, and I found some in them. Finally, my way of looking at them changed so much that I left nearly in love with all these ugly girls."

Because of their abilities, many of these young girls eventually married into wealthy and established families. The ones who were not as talented musically still earned an excellent education and usually wound up staying at the Pietà as nuns and teaching the younger girls. A few of the exceptional girls opted not to get married and stayed on at the Pietà as mild celebrities.

By the time Vivaldi was hired at the Pietà, the all-girl orchestra was already famous, drawing huge crowds to their performances. Unlike the girls, Vivaldi was in full view of the audience when he conducted and he took advantage of the prominence this position afforded him. More than any other composer who had worked for the Pietà before, Vivaldi used the girls to showcase his works. Then he would offer those works for sale to the nobility that frequented the Pietà performances.

This was a successful strategy. Over the next five years Vivaldi became popular with audiences. People began showing up at Pietà concerts specifically to hear Vivaldi's compositions and to witness the amazing skills he had taught the violinists. To further his popularity, he accepted all invitations to play violin at the grand estates of any admirer with money to lavish upon him. This included performing for the French Ambassador in 1705 and the Austrian Ambassador in 1707. He even conducted the girls before King Frederick IV of Denmark and Norway. When he learned that the king had been entertained by his work, Vivaldi wrote a letter to him:

> Enviable is the fate of a humble heart if it is forced, when it meets a sovereign great by birth, but even greater by virtue, to ensure the multiplicity of his tributes, whatever they are. That truth obliges my intellect to reflect upon the heroic spirit of Your Majesty, so well known to the world, and it gives me great confidence to offer you my abasement which in real consideration of my nothingness could not in any way be more diminished.

Vivaldi's letters were always written in such a manner, overflowing with praise for the recipient and depicting himself as deeply humble. This fawning humility was the fashion of the times. Vivaldi actually took great pride in his work and did not hesitate to write to people with power, such as the king. In his letter, Vivaldi dedicated to the king the piece he had so enjoyed hearing—Opus 2, twelve sonatas for violin and harpsichord.

There was one big problem in Vivaldi's new job. It was the obligation of every priest to take part in Mass, a church service central to the religion. In the early 1700s, Mass was a ritual involving music and prayer that lasted from three to six hours. The priests were required to stand the entire service. Due to his persistent illness, Vivaldi found this experience too taxing. Finally, he decided that he would not celebrate (or officiate at)

Mass. In a letter he wrote later in his life, Vivaldi explained:

> I have not now said mass for twenty-five years, and I shall never do so again… on account of an ailment I have suffered from since birth, which oppresses me greatly. When I had just been ordained a priest, I still said mass for rather more than a year and then gave it up because three times I had to leave the altar without finishing mass on account of my illness.

Normally a priest would not be exempted from one of the most significant rites of the church but Vivaldi was given a great deal of freedom within his position at the Pietà because of his great talent and the revenue he brought in through the concerts.

The Pietà board of governors made every decision about how the school should be run. They spent the money, decided which children would be accepted into the school, sorted out which girls were talented enough to be promoted into music studies, chose who would be hired to work at the Pietà, and defined the duties each job would entail. After Vivaldi's first year at the Pietà, the board of governors, pleased with his early achievements, decided to raise his salary. "Since the sustained efforts of Don Antonio Vivaldi, the girls' violin teacher, have borne fruit," they wrote, "it is moved that forty ducats be added to his normal salary … so that he may be encouraged in his tasks and for the greater profit of the girls."

Each year, the governing review board gathered to

analyze the worth of Vivaldi's position and to decide whether or not they wanted him to stay. In 1709, when Vivaldi was thirty-one years old, the governors suddenly changed their minds about Vivaldi's value and voted to not keep him. While Antonio Vivaldi would wind up working at the Pio Ospedale della Pietà off and on over the course of thirty-six years, his first term of employment lasted only seven.

There are many speculations as to why the governors decided to let Vivaldi go. It is especially odd that he was fired during Carnival. The biggest celebration in every Italian city, Carnival was a sweeping, decadent festival that began the day after Christmas and culminated with the grandest spectacles the day before Ash Wednesday, which marks the beginning of lent in the Catholic Church. Venice became especially busy during Carnival. It was critical that every theater have a full season of operas

A procession in the *Piazetta San Marco*, leading into the beautiful and ornate St. Mark's Chapel. *(By Gentile Bellini, courtesy of Adademia, Venice.)*

Wearing masks was a popular Venetian custom, not limited to the time of Carnival. *(Painting by Pietro Longhi, courtesy of Rezzonico, Venice.)*

and concerts to draw paying visitors. Since Carnival was based on a religious event, the churches got involved by creating spectacles to draw people to their services. For example, before High Mass, twenty-two chaplains of St. Mark's would put on long church garments made of gold cloth and ceremoniously escort the doge (the leader) of Venice from his palace to the church. Seeing the splendor and pomp, people would join in the procession, expecting even more of a display once they got inside the church doors.

The Pietà would have needed Vivaldi's services during Carnival more than ever, to get music ready for the girls to perform and to conduct the orchestra at the many events that would take place over the four months of festivities. It stands to reason that they must have been extremely displeased with Vivaldi to fire him at such a critical time.

Some historians believe that Vivaldi was receiving too much notoriety in the secular world for work originally written for the Pietà orchestra. The Church did not want to have to compete for his attention. They might have felt he cared more about his fame and public performances than teaching and writing for the girls. It is possible he offended his superiors by refusing to celebrate Mass. To many people, Vivaldi's priestly responsibilities should have taken priority over his musical pursuits, rather than the other way around.

Whatever the reason for his dismissal, Antonio Vivaldi did not pine for the Pietà. Instead, he relished the newfound fame he had received as a composer and violinist. He took some time in his first year away from the orphanage to travel around Italy playing concerts, basking in his fame, and earning money.

In 1710, Vivaldi returned to Venice to be in the presence of the composer George Frideric Handel, whom the Italians nicknamed *Il Sassone* after his German hometown of Saxony. Handel was by far the most popular musical figure of his time. Many considered him to be a genius. His operas were played to enormous acclaim and Vivaldi no doubt hoped to have a little of Handel's

George Frideric Handel, in a portrait from 1756. This German composer would have much success in Italy. *(Paiting by Phillippe Mercier, private collection of Viscount Fitzmarriso.)*

greatness rub off on him. Handel had come to Italy at the age of twenty-one, and now, four years later, he brought his highly anticipated opera *Agrippina* to Venice. The story of this opera is an account of Agrippina, the conniving wife of the Roman emperor Claudius, who used the rumors of her husband's death to secure the throne for her son, Nero.

According to surviving records from the *Teatro San Angelo* in Venice, Antonio Vivaldi was on the pay ledger as a violinist at the theater during the time *Agrippina* was in town. He must have been a featured player in the orchestra. This would have normally been a job beneath his level of fame and ability, but he likely took the

Title page of the libretto for Handel's *Agrippina,* from the 1709 performance in Vienna.

position in order to work with and meet Handel. This was probably his first real taste of the theatrical structure of operatic music. Vivaldi also learned about the large sums of money opera composers could earn. Handel, a composer almost ten years younger than Vivaldi, earned a salary that dwarfed anything the orphanage could ever pay. The idea of earning such fees, not to mention the respect and adoration of the public, must have excited Vivaldi.

Opera would have to wait, however. On September 27, 1711, Vivaldi's secular pursuits were put on hold once again when the review board at the Pietà came calling:

> Realizing the necessity of securing ever better instrumental tuition for the girls studying music in order to increase the reputation of this pious establishment, the post of violin master being vacant, we move that Don Antonio Vivaldi be appointed violin master…

The director of music, Francesco Gasparini had become very ill, and they needed someone to help out with the compositions. Despite Vivaldi's flaws as a priest, he was the only ordained musician in Venice talented enough for the position. The governors offered him a pay raise to go with his new position and Vivaldi accepted. Although he now dreamed of a career in opera production, he was practical enough to know he was not yet ready to tackle the theatrical world. Returning to the Pietà was more prestigious, and lucrative, than playing violin in the orchestra pit at the San Angelo Theater.

At thirty-three, Vivaldi had more work to do than ever before. The governors listed what they needed from him: "Two new Mass and Vespers [afternoon services] settings annually; at least two motets every month; occasional compositions as required for funerals…" and the list goes on. Vivaldi had to write a lot of music at incredible speed. Over the course of his time at the Pietà he composed more than five hundred pieces of music.

Even with this highly revered position and huge

workload, Vivaldi could no longer be satisfied at the orphanage. He was now aware of the greater opportunities the music world had to offer.

Chapter Three
Operas and Concertos

Vivaldi wanted his music to reach an audience beyond Venice. He knew the best way to get his name and melodies before European music lovers would be to go on tour and play it himself, but this was hardly an option for Vivaldi. Traveling during this period was an arduous task that could only be done by horse and carriage. There were few paved roads, and lengthy excursions could only be undertaken during good weather. Getting to countries such as England and France could take weeks. Vivaldi's constant poor health made the prospect of touring even more dire. So, in 1711, Vivaldi chose his next best option and decided it was time to publish the scores of his concertos and other instrumental pieces originally written for the Pietà.

Venetian publishers used moveable type to print their

books. The German Johann Gutenberg had invented this method of printing in 1450. Letters were punched and engraved into copper molds that were filled with molten metal. The letters were all uniform in size and spacing so that they could be interchanged to make different words. To print a page, the letters making up each word were placed on a printing plate by hand. The plate was covered in ink and paper was pressed onto it. The raised letters then left their imprint on the paper. Once the requisite number of pages was printed, the letters were rearranged to form the next page. The Germans refined this skill and brought it to Venice in 1469. For the next two hundred years, printing became one of Venice's most profitable industries.

Unfortunately, this process was sloppy and imprecise when it came to printing music. Music written on a page

A printing press at work in 1642.

Here, a page from Vivaldi's Opus 2 violin sonatas is written out in an early method of music printing. Notice that each note is given its own individual tail. *(Courtesy of Venice Conservatorio di Musica.)*

looks like circles imposed over a staff of five parallel lines. Some of the circles are open, some closed; some have an ascending or descending vertical line, some have none. The placement of the circle on or between lines determines which note to play. Music printed by Guttenberg's method was messy and difficult to read. In Amsterdam, a man named Estienne Roger had recently developed a new technique for printing music. Roger worked by engraving sequences of notes on full-sized plates, rather than moving around individual notes.

Roger's manuscripts were much more expensive to

Roger's method of printing music became popular for its cleanliness and the ease with which it accurately reproduced scores. This is the first violin part from the "Winter" section of Vivaldi's *Four Seasons. (Courtesy of Venice Conservatorio di Musica.)*

produce, but musicians preferred reading the clearer type. If the players were pleased with the music copy, they would play it more often, an idea that appealed to Vivaldi. Roger also had the foresight to number the pages and to order the works, which served to help collectors later on. The Venetian publishers ignored these details, since they did not see any demand for collections of music.

The most important thing about Roger's printing process was that his publications could easily be re-printed. Guttenberg's method required each note to be reset. But Roger's engraved plates were permanent and could easily be re-inked and printed. In an age when there was no such thing as copyright or property laws protecting creative works, this feature of Roger's publishing was important. If someone could buy a clear reprint from Roger they might not spend money on a stolen, cheap, messy copy, and Vivaldi would earn more royalty payments for his work.

Wanting his works documented in the best way possible, Vivaldi chose to send his music to far-away Amsterdam instead of having it published locally. He was the first Venetian to have his music published in Northern Europe. After seeing Vivaldi's beautiful and easily reproduced scores, other composers in Venice began to sending their work to Roger in Amsterdam. This helped Roger flourish, while the Venetian publishers gradually went out of business.

The first of Vivaldi's works printed by Roger was his Opus 3, *L'Estro Armonico (The Musical Inspiration)*. It was one of the largest collections of concertos ever created, so big it filled two volumes. Many were originally written for the *Pietà*. In the introduction, Vivaldi wrote, "I must... confess that in the past my compositions... have been subjected... to a poor standard of printing. Now they will have the major advantage of being engraved by the celebrated hand of Monsieur Estienne Roger... Keep me in your kind remembrance and be happy."

The *Armonico* was a quick success. Musicians all over Europe became fascinated with the concertos. The collection came to define how Baroque concertos ought to work. Corelli's *concerto grossi* format was replaced by Vivaldi's new pattern of three movements: an initial fast-paced movement followed by a slow one, and the concluding third movement that returned to the quick pace of the first. Vivaldi's concertos also differed from Corelli's by featuring a soloist who stood away from the rest of the ensemble, and who engaged in a lively duel

A French printing shop. Paris would, along with Amsterdam, become an important center for the printing and distribution of music. *(Courtesy of Bulloz Photographic Collection, Paris.)*

with the larger orchestra. Corelli's concertino groups had merely played counterpoint to the orchestra, as if the melody were the ball in a game of catch. Vivaldi made sure there were passages in his compositions that allowed the soloists to show off their virtuosity. This dramatic use of varying speed, volume, and dynamics made Vivaldi's work more lively and exciting than earlier Baroque music.

Vivaldi's concertos were so popular that Italian composers who were older and more established than Vivaldi, such as Evaristo Felice dall'Abaco and Tomaso Albinoni, adopted his concerto format in the middle of their careers. In fact, most of Italy favored the new style, and the Vivaldi concerto form was also accepted enthusiastically in Paris, France. Only in Rome, which was Corelli's home and fairly conservative, did musicians hold tightly to the Corellian style of the concerto grossi. Corelli died two years after the *Armonico* was published, and his death ended the adherence to the old form. Vivaldi's concerto format came to define the concerto as it is known today.

Musicians in Germany were particularly taken with *L'Estro Armonico*. While concertos were a well-known form in Italy, in Northern Europe sonatas had been the preferred form of music. Sonatas were also multi-movement works, but they were performed by a small ensemble rather than by a full orchestra. These small ensembles played what came to be called chamber music because it was generally performed in the homes (chambers) of the wealthy. Subsequently, there were few con-

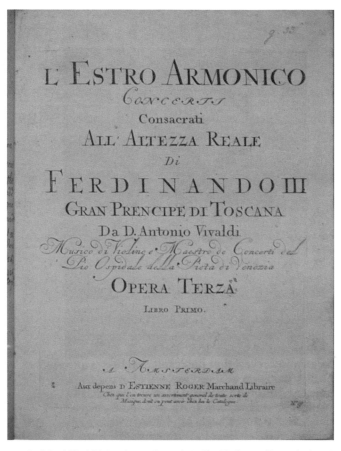

Title page for Vivaldi's *L'Estro Armonico,* printed by Estienne Roger in Amsterdam in 1711. *(Courtesy of British Library.)*

cert halls large enough for full orchestras in Northern Europe. All the same, when the Roger publication of *Armonico* introduced the concerto to the German territories, it quickly caught on.

Prince Johann Ernst of Saxe-Weimer copied Vivaldi's style for concertos of his own. German musicians such as Gottfried Heinrich Stölzel, Johann David Heinichen, and Johann Georg Pisendel came to Venice to find

Vivaldi and study with him. In return, Vivaldi learned from his German visitors a love of woodwind instruments and became one of the few Italian composers to write concertos for the oboe, bassoon, flute, and recorder.

Another German musician who was influenced by Vivaldi lived in Saxony. Johann Sebastian Bach was slightly younger than Vivaldi, twenty-six to Vivaldi's thirty-five. Bach, though already on the road to musical fame, wrote primarily for the Protestant Church, so it is

Johann Sebastian Bach. *(Courtesy of Museum für Geschichte der Stadt Leipzig.)*

unlikely that Vivaldi knew any of his music. Bach, however, had certainly heard Vivaldi's. He even arranged six of the pieces from *Armonico* for harpsichord, an instrument similar to, and a predecessor of, the piano.

To arrange music means to take the melody, or theme, of a piece of music and change the instrumentation, the speed (or tempo) it is played at, or even to alter the rhythm itself. Bach's arrangement of Vivaldi's music was intended as a compliment and served to make the *Armonico* even more accessible to other musicians in Europe. Far more people knew how to play harpsichord than violin, and Bach's arrangements called for fewer musicians, which made assembling performances an easier task.

The same year Bach was reworking Vivaldi's music in faraway Saxony, important events were happening in Vivaldi's life. At the Pietà, Gasparini quit for good, and Vivaldi officially took over his job. The review board promoted him over another Pietà composer named Pietro Dall'Olio, who did not write music quickly enough to become the leading house composer.

Despite his promotion, and all the new responsibilities that came with it, Vivaldi could not attend to work right away. He already had plans for that spring. He arranged to take a couple months away from the Pietà in order to take a step toward a new career. He was going to stage the world premiere of his first opera.

A favorite diversion of people in early eighteenth-century Venice was attending the opera. Nearly a century earlier the first full-length opera, a drama with dialogue sung from beginning to end, had been staged in Mantua, Italy. *Orfeo,* written by Claudio Monteverdi, was presented in 1607 for a private performance before the Duke of Mantua. Operas continued to be private affairs until 1639, when a staging in Rome of Monteverdi's *Adone* became the first opera performance open to the public. With tunes that were easy to hum and

MONTEVERDI AND THE ORIGINS OF OPERA

Claudio Monteverdi (1567-1643) was a strong-willed and passionate musician and composer who traveled widely through Europe, mostly with his employer, the Duke of Mantua, Vincenzo Gonzaga. These journeys exposed Monteverdi to a variety of events, people, customs, composers, and styles of music, and reinforced his belief that music was meant to express emotion. In 1607, experimenting with the ideas and techniques of other musicians, Monteverdi wrote *Orfeo,* which is considered the first 'modern' opera. Based on the Greek myth of Orpheus and Euridice, this opera, like other early instances of the form, sprang out of a return to the principles, themes, and techniques of Greek theater.

Monteverdi called *Orfeo* a *favola en musica* or a 'story in music.' He tried to have his music interpret the poetry of the libretto. He wrote about people and their feelings—about love, hate, death, life, war, and peace. Monteverdi went on to become maestro di cappella at St. Mark's Cathedral in Venice. He is credited with being the father of modern opera.

The earliest operas were performed only rarely, and then exclusively for private audiences made up of royalty and their guests. Opera began evolving into more of a public form of entertainment around 1639, when the first commercial opera houses opened in Venice. After this point, opera became a key ingredient in the musical culture of Italy and, soon, all of Europe.

A Venetian painting of an *intermezzo,* the short, comic operatic work performed between two parts of a dramatic opera. *(Courtesy of Teatrale alla Scala, Milan.)*

lyrics that could make people laugh or weep, opera quickly became the most popular entertainment of the era. By Vivaldi's time there were as many as six commercial opera houses in Venice, each producing at least six operas per year.

These productions were grand affairs, with the average opera lasting four hours. People did not attend opera just for the music. More important than the singers, orchestra, and scenery of the opera was the social experience surrounding it. Aristocrats went in order to show the poor that they supported the arts, and the poor went because the tickets were inexpensive. The audience used the occasion as a time to enjoy the company of friends and family. Talking and eating throughout the performances was common behavior. The music was often merely a backdrop to the audience's socializing.

Antonio Vivaldi had tasted the life of the performer early on when he played violin duets with his father and appeared at St. Mark's. When he played in the orchestra for Handel's *Agrippina*, he experienced an opera production firsthand. The rustle of costumes, the gorgeous voices, and the dynamic scenery all appealed to him, as did the large salary. Although he received sixty ducats a year teaching and composing at the Pietà, he could earn two hundred ducats for staging one opera. His name would be on the lips of every person in Venice. Even for a man of the cloth, the prospect of fame and riches was too much to resist.

For the performance of Vivaldi's first opera, *Ottone in Villa*, he went to Vicenza, a town north of Venice. The impresario, or producer, in the smaller town was willing to bet that Vivaldi would be a successful operatic composer. But he was not willing to take that gamble in one of the more important Venice theaters.

The impresario was also taking a gamble on the librettist, or storywriter. Sebastiano Binacardi, working under the alias of Domenico Lalli because he was hiding from the police, wrote the lyrics. Nervous as he was about both the composer and librettist, the impresario had faith in the story, a comedic romp with the kind of silly plot that tended to go over well with audiences.

Ottone is a comedy about a fictitious Roman emperor in a romantic dilemma. The woman he loves, Cleonilla, takes advantage of him, while stringing along two other men at the same time. This farcical comedy is filled with deceptions, misunderstandings, forged love letters, and characters in disguise. Vivaldi employs common operatic conventions of the time to tell his story. For instance, the entire story takes place over the course of one day, and the arias (vocal solos) are used to illustrate a character's mood rather than to describe events.

Staging an opera was more complicated than the work Vivaldi had done before. At the Pietà, he composed alone and had obedient students to follow his direction. When writing opera, he had to compose with a librettist and deal with a huge number of temperaments, including those of the set designers, lighting designers, costumers, opera divas, and investors in the production. The usual bravado Vivaldi felt about his work deserted him during this first attempt at an opera. Often when a composer found weaknesses in the libretto or text of the opera, he would modify the lyrics to match his music, for the music was considered to be more important than the contrived storyline. In this case, the text for *Ottone* did not suit Vivaldi's musical ideas, but he held back his impulse to change it. He forced his composition to fit. Years later he would rewrite this opera, but at this time he did not feel confident enough to alter Lalli's writing. Although the opera had the weaknesses of a first attempt, it also had many strengths.

A young opera singer in Venice, mid-1700s.
(Courtesy of Civico Museo Bibliografico Musicale, Bologna.)

The arias were by far the highlight. Arias were usually written in a simple format and scattered throughout, much like songs in a contemporary musical. They consisted of an opening melody, a contrasting middle, and a repetition of the opening melody. That repeated melody gave the opera singers a chance to show off their vocal ability. During the third section of the aria, singers were able to improvise with trills, runs, and scales over the tune. These moments did not advance the plot of the opera, but they were the vocal equivalent of fireworks and often gave insight as to the character's mood or motivation. Vivaldi may have been an inexperienced operatic composer, but he knew enough to fill his first opera with dynamic, crowd-pleasing arias.

The audiences did not seem to mind the flaws of *Ottone in Villa*. It was a great success after it opened in May of 1713. People turned out to see what the priest of the Pio Ospedale della Pietà, known as a composer of concertos for talented students and religious services,

sphere. Surely the presence of nuns and orphaned girls was a relief after a month or two of temperamental divas and production hassles.

Somehow Vivaldi managed to do it all. He taught the girls, wrote pieces for them to perform, and conducted their concerts, while also composing operas and publishing music collections. In 1715, his duties at the Pietà were increased again, so that each year he had to compose an entire Mass, a Vespers, an oratorio, and over thirty motets (polyphonic vocal pieces), in addition to his previous responsibilities. (Oratorios were religious choral versions of operas that used a similar dramatic structure without the elaborate scenery and staging.)

The first oratorio he created, *Moyses Deus Pharaonis,* was a recounting of the Biblical story in which Moses confronts the Egyptian pharaoh Ramses. Two years later he wrote another oratorio, titled *Juditha Triumphans*. In this story, King Nebuchadnezzer has sent his Assyrian army, led by the barbaric Holofernes, to punish Jews who have not paid the king tribute. Judith, a Jewish woman, tricks Holofernes and, in so doing, saves her city and fellow Jews from destruction. Judith offers to betray her city by telling Holofernes the safest way to enter and conquer it. Holofernes believes victory is at hand. Before laying siege to Judith's city, he attempts to woo her with a fine meal, planning to seduce her in his tent afterwards. Judith, for her part, makes sure the general has plenty to drink, then foils his plans when she kills Holofernes by beheading him. Judith returns to her town

The grisly Biblical story of Judith and Holofernes inspired not only Vivaldi's oratorio, but many other works of art as well. In Artemisa Gentileschi's painting, from 1620, Judith performs the heroic act with strength and determination. *(Courtesy of Uffizi, Florence.)*

with the head of Holofernes in hand, and the Assyrian soldiers flee. With her brave act, Judith saved her town and fellow Jews from destruction by the Assyrians.

Vivaldi wrote this second oratorio for patriotic as well as religious reasons. Venice and the Ottoman Empire (the Turks) had engaged in a series of wars in the middle of the fifteenth century. After Constantinople finally fell to the Turks in 1453, Venice joined an alliance formed to stop their advance into Europe. At the peak of the city's influence, during the Renaissance, Venice was the dominant power in the anti-Ottoman alliance. The Turkish advance in Eastern Europe was finally stopped, although at one point, in 1683, they laid siege to Vienna, Austria. Finally, in August 1716, the decisive battle of this long series of conflicts arrived when the Turks attacked the Venetian controlled island of Corfu.

THE OTTOMAN EMPIRE

The Ottoman Empire was born out of the long struggle between the Muslims of Anatolia and the last Eastern remnant of the Roman Empire, the shrinking Christian Byzantine state. The name Ottoman is taken from the name of the family—Osmanli, in Turkish—that ruled the empire from the thirteenth to the twentieth century.

The Ottoman Empire reached its peak of military and cultural achievement during the rule of Sultan Süleyman the Magnificent, from 1520 until 1566. Süleyman doubled the size of the Empire until it reached from Vienna in the west to the Arab Peninsula in the east, and from the Crimean Sea in the north, all the way south to present day Sudan.

Located in the center of valuable trade routes, at its peak the Ottoman Empire was the most wealthy kingdom in the world. The population was well educated and cosmopolitan. Although the Empire was the political center of the Islamic world, Süleyman and other rulers developed a legacy of religious toleration unlike any that existed in Western Europe. Jews, Christians and Muslims flourished, although there was no modern separation of church and state.

Grand buildings and Islamic temples were built during

Süleyman's reign; vast amounts of money were invested in education, art and public buildings. Ottoman science and literature was the envy of the west. Today, the Ottoman Empire is credited with keeping the great achievements of the ancient world, including Classical Greece, alive over the long period between the fall of Rome and the birth of the European Renaissance.

Vivaldi and his librettist wrote *Juditha* during this uncertain time, before they knew the outcome of the battle. Vivaldi hoped that Venice would echo Judith's triumph and win at Corfu. His oratorio became a patriotic anthem and, when word arrived that the Venetians had defeated the Turks, this inspirational piece was played to enormous acclaim.

Juditha is not the only powerful and popular oratorio Vivaldi wrote, but it is one of the few that survives. While his concerto collections were published in Amsterdam, and his sacred works were stored in a library at the *Pietà*, no one published his operatic pieces. Music was published only for personal use, not for study, as it is today, and only works that could be performed by individuals or small groups were needed on paper.

Vivaldi's cravings for fame and fortune led him to the opera house where he hoped his writing would earn him the respect he desired. It is a sad truth, though, that while Vivaldi wrote at least forty-seven operas, only nineteen survive intact. Despite his conviction that opera would make him a success, much of his operatic legacy has been lost.

Over the course of centuries, Turkey and Venice engaged in many battles. This seventeenth-century painting depicts one in which Venetian soldiers repossess a fortress that had earlier fallen to the Turks. Below, the Turkish boats, on the left, are overtaken by the Venetians. *(Courtesy of Biblioteca del Civico Museo Correr, Venice.)*

Chapter Four
The Music Business

A great deal of money could be made in the music business and Antonio Vivaldi was not shy about attempting to get his share. Although ticket prices for the opera might have been cheap enough for even the poor to attend, Vivaldi, being an enterprising young man, set his sights on wooing audiences from the noble houses of Europe. When the wealthy came to his shows, they often brought gifts or invitations to visit their courts, which often led to earning extra money. The Italian elite had a powerful influence on theatrical events.

In the early days of opera, seating in the theaters was very uncomfortable. Wealthy opera attendees arranged to have box seats added to the larger houses like the *Teatro San Giovanni Grisostomo.* Once comfortable boxes were in place, the theater became a more prestigious place to socialize. The opera became not only a setting to hear music, but somewhere a person had to be seen in order to fit into high Venetian society.

The rich also had control over which musicians succeeded and which did not. If they did not like a composer or singer, that artist would not be able to find employment. To get in the good graces of a powerful duke, prince, or king guaranteed a steady career. Once a nobleman (or his wife, mother, or lover) began to dote on a particular composer, that composer could count on years of well-paid work writing for the noble and his court.

Vivaldi learned the politics of music early on. His exposure to the music business as a child taught him more than how to play the violin, for he was dedicating

Teatro San Giovanni Grisostamo, in Venice. The theater was one of the seven in the lagoon city dedicated solely to opera. *(Courtesy of Civici Musei Veneziani d'Arte e di Storia, Venice.)*

his music to powerful men from the very beginning—his Opus 1 went to the Venetian nobleman Count Gambara, for example. Vivaldi dedicated his first published work, the *Armonico,* to Grand Prince Ferdinand III of Tuscany. "Let this small tribute of my humblest devotion remain what it actually is," he wrote. "I know that you look not upon that what is offered but on the real humility of the one who offers it and I can have full confidence in the infinite graciousness of your elevated mind which spurns nothing and welcomes all."

The purpose of a dedication was to make a nobleman think that a work had been written expressly for him. This act personalized the music and made the recipient feel special enough to want to purchase more work from the artist, or perhaps take the artist under his wing and become his patron. This way the wealthy felt they made a vital contribution to the arts. Vivaldi's dedications were always full of flowery words and puffed up with flattery, such as this dedication to Prince Ferdinand: "The opus may gain but little approval from your knowledgeable, formidable and truly sovereign judgment, but it is offered with all the devotion of a humble heart to the boundless merit of Your Royal Highness, although it bears no proportion to your venerable greatness."

Such fawning adoration swelled the heads of the European aristocrats, and each man who received such a dedication quickly ranked Vivaldi among his favorite composers. Noblemen would show off their signed manuscripts to impress guests. This helped to build

Vivaldi's circle of influence and guarantee his presence on the Venetian scene.

Vivaldi knew how to push for more business. When Herr von Uffenbach, an engineer and music lover, invited Vivaldi to his home after dinner one evening, Vivaldi turned the German visitor's request for one grand concerto into a more profitable order for ten concertos, which he delivered within three days. He also offered Uffenbach violin lessons.

Charles de Brosses was the first President of the *Parlement* of Dijon, in France. He traveled extensively in Italy from 1739-40 and wrote of Vivaldi, "[He] became my intimate friend so as to sell me some concertos at a very high price. In part, he succeeded; but I too got what I wanted, which was to hear him and to have frequent hours of good musical recreation."

In 1716, Antonio Vivaldi's importance in the music world reached a new height when Friedrich August III, future King of Poland, came to Venice to seek him out. He brought with him an entourage that included the German violinist Johann Georg Pisendel. Vivaldi was hired to tutor young Pisendel at the violin. Busy schedule or not, Vivaldi would have been a fool to turn down such an opportunity. Being in good graces with another king meant more work.

Vivaldi relished in the connection he made with Pisendel. He wrote six concertos and three sonatas for his pupil. A year later, at Friedrich's request, Pisendel tackled a violin concerto by Vivaldi at an opera performance in Venice. His playing was full of an ornamental style that reflected the training he received from the violin master. August III was pleased that his money had been well spent.

That same year Vivaldi also tutored Daniel Gottlibe Treu, a German composer who had been sent to Venice by his employer, the Duke of Würtemberg. It is speculated that composers Johann David Heinichen of Germany and Jan Dismas Zelenka of Bohemia may have been Vivaldi's pupils during this time, as well. His influence is evident in their compositions.

One of the main reasons Vivaldi accepted so many jobs, and worked so hard for high-paying benefactors, was because the fees earned from his published work proved disappointing. Venice had such a thirst for music that the orchestral pieces he wrote for the Pietà and elsewhere were rarely performed more than twice. The works quickly became familiar, and audiences were more eager to attend a musical event that offered a new Vivaldi piece than to hear a familiar concerto, even if *that* piece had been new just the week before. Publishing the pieces seemed the logical way to keep the work alive. That way, the old pieces could be performed in places outside of Venice for audiences who had not yet become bored with it. Unfortunately, due to an abundance of pirated copies of his material, Vivaldi could not earn a living from the sales of his printed music. His belief that the Roger's publications would deter people from purchasing pirated copies proved wrong, and it made much more business sense now for Vivaldi to sell his works privately to kings and princes for a large sum up front.

Vivaldi's business sense extended to the theater as well. He realized how much an opera with his name attached to it was worth, and he steadily increased his commission fees as the years went by. To gain control over the production of his operas and dictate how money was spent, he became an impresario instead of handing the job over to someone else. He also earned a higher salary if he conducted his operas. Of course, this meant he had to be present and involved in the staging.

As his work became more and more popular with audiences and noble courts, Vivaldi found he had to travel to the opera theaters throughout Italy and the great courts of Europe. He decided to take a leave of absence from teaching at the Pietà for a few years to pursue his outside interests. In April of 1718, Vivaldi, now almost forty years old, took his most recent opera, *Armida al campo d'Egitto*, to Mantua, an Italian city west of Venice.

"I was at Mantua for three years in the service of the exceedingly God fearing Prince of Darmstadt," Vivaldi wrote in a letter. He was there at the request of Prince Philip of Hessen-Darmstadt, the Governor of Mantua. Prince Philip, an avid music lover, wanted Vivaldi as his *maestro di cappella di camera* (court composer).

Although he primarily wrote music for Prince Philip, including an opera for the Carnival season and several secular vocal works, during this time, Vivaldi had other obligations to uphold as well. In the three years he spent in Mantua he also had two operas playing in Venice, two in Vicenza, and two in Milan. On top of that, he still composed pieces for the Pietà.

In fact, to guarantee that Vivaldi did not shirk on his responsibility to the Pietà, the board of governors made a new agreement "…with the aforementioned Vivaldi to deliver, as he proposes to do, two concertos every month for the time when he is himself in Venice, and during the time of his absence to send these by messenger if this can be done without any special increase in the cost of transmission." The same agreement contracted him to rehearse with the young musicians at least three times if he was in town.

On January 19, 1720, the Empress in Vienna, Eleonore Magdaleno Theresa, widow of Leopold I, died. Out of respect, all theaters within the Austrian Empire, which included Mantua, were temporarily closed. With no work to be had, there was no point in Vivaldi staying.

Mantua had been just the beginning of his travels to meet and work for people of great influence. Vivaldi returned to Venice only for a short stay before moving on to Rome in 1723. There he staged his opera *Ercole sul Termodonte* at the Teatro Capranica. The libretto, set in the Orient, was written by a Roman member of the clergy named Don Giacomo Francesco Bussani. In Rome, women were not permitted to sing in the opera, so all of the female roles had to be played by *castrati*—male singers who had been castrated at an early age to prevent their beautifully high voices from changing. Vivaldi spent three Carnival seasons in Rome and, according to his letters, played twice before the Pope. He had at least one opera per year performed there between 1723 and 1725.

During his stay in Rome, Pier Leone Ghezzi, a famous artist who painted caricatures, drew a portrait of Vivaldi that exaggerated his facial features. Several portraits

P. L. Ghezzi's caricature of Vivaldi, the redheaded priest. *(Courtesy of Biblioteca Apostolica Vaticana.)*

had been painted of the red-headed priest in his lifetime, including a painting by G. B. Martini of an anonymous music master that could not be anyone but Vivaldi because of the lock of red hair poking out from under the powdered wig. Of all the paintings and sketches, Ghezzi's small drawing is said to reflect Vivaldi's character more than any other. The uplifted head with the strong jaw and prominent nose raised ever so slightly in the air expresses a confidence that borders on arrogance. Yet his eyes have a feeling of gentleness about them and his mouth is slightly open, as if he is asking for approval. The sketch depicts the desire to please that had remained with Vivaldi since he was a sickly little boy in his father's barbershop.

Near the end of his stay in Rome, forty-seven year old Antonio Vivaldi wrote his most famous instrumental work. Opus VIII, *Il cimento dell'armonia e dell'inventione*, opens with four concertos that represent the seasons of the year. This group of concertos is now called *The Four Seasons*.

The Four Seasons is program music, which means that it is supposed to create specific emotions and thoughts within the listener. The need to have the music communicate the program, or idea, that is usually implied by the title, restrains the composer. During his life, Vivaldi wrote a number of such works, often based on poetry or paintings. *The Four Seasons* attempts to capture the experience of each of the seasons and is based upon four sonnets on the same theme. Even though

Vivaldi's *Four Seasons* concertos provide a musical counterpart to this painting, "Apollo Leading the Dance of the Four Seasons to the Music of Time." *(Courtesy of Rainsville Archive.)*

Vivaldi is not known for being a poet, it is believed that he wrote these poems before composing the music to depict them in sound. The goal was to create a narrative that used music instead of words.

SPRING
Spring has come and with it gaiety,
The birds salute it with joyous song,
And the brooks, caressed by Zephyr's breath,
Flow meanwhile with sweet murmurings:

The sky is covered with dark clouds,
Announced by lightning and thunder.
But when they are silenced, the little birds
Return to fill the air with their song:

Then does the meadow, in full flower,
Ripple with its leafy plants.
The goat-herd dozes, guarded by his faithful dog.

Rejoicing in the pastoral bagpipes,
Nymphs and Shepherds dance, in love,
Their faces glowing with Springtime's brilliance.

In the Spring section of *The Four Seasons*, Vivaldi illustrates the "woof *woof*" cadence of barking dogs with the use of loud and rasping violas. Violin runs represent rippling brooks. The violins also chirp out birdcalls, while the soloist represents lightning during a storm. Finally the violins are muted and played as though in imitation of bagpipes, to introduce the sound of a rustic dance. Being a Vivaldi concerto, the music is divided into three movements that reflect the movement of the poem—from soft birdsongs, to a sudden spring storm, to the joyous dance with all of spring's accompanying brilliant sounds.

SUMMER
Under the heavy season of a burning sun,
Man languishes, his herd wilts, the pine is parched
The cuckoo finds its voice, and chiming in with it
The turtle-dove, the goldfinch.

Zephyr breathes gently but, contested,
The North-wind appears nearby and suddenly:
The shepherd sobs because, uncertain,

Previous page: A summer storm, much like the one described in the summer section of Vivaldi's *Four Seasons*. *(Detail of "La Tempesta," by Giorgione.)*

He fears the wild squall and its effects:

His weary limbs have no repose, goaded by
His fear of lightning and wild thunder;
While gnats and flies in furious swarms surround him.

Alas, his fears prove all too grounded,
Thunder and lightning split the Heavens, and hail-
    stones
Slice the top of the corn and other grain.

The opening of this concerto is bold and breathless,
reflecting summer's oppressive heat. As the piece un-
folds, one hears more birds, including a cuckoo in the
bass line, turtledoves and a goldfinch in the trills of
violins. The full orchestra enters, bringing with it the
cold north winds and the first of a series of storms.

AUTUMN
The country-folk celebrate, with dance and song,
The joy of gathering a bountiful harvest.
With Bacchus's liquor, quaffed liberally,
Their joy finishes in slumber.

Each one renounces dance and song
The mild air is pleasant
And the season invites ever increasingly
To savor a sweet slumber

The hunters at dawn go to the hunt,
With horns and guns and dogs they sally forth,
The beasts flee, their trail is followed:

Already dismay'd and exhausted, from the great noise
Of guns and dogs, threaten'd with wounds,
They flee, languishing, and die, cowering.

The Autumn concerto is full of fun, with sections that mimic the dances and songs that peasants enjoyed. This frivolity is accompanied by the drinking of wine and ale, and Vivaldi illustrates this with a violin solo that depicts a stumbling drunken man. He uses syncopations, or unexpectedly placed rhythmic accents, to express the drunk's hiccups. The movement draws to a close as the revelry concludes.

The next movement is all about the deep, fulfilling slumber that comes after a night of drink and merriment. Then, in Autumn's final movement, the hunt that is indicated in the poem is rousingly portrayed. This movement features violins imitating the call of the hunting horn. Vivaldi depicts animals fleeing from hunter's gunshots, but not quickly enough to escape the hunters and their baying hounds.

WINTER
Frozen and trembling among the chilly snow,
Our breathing hampered by horrid winds,
As we run, we stamp our feet continuously,
Our teeth chatter with the frightful cold:

We move to the fire and contented peace,
While the rain outside pours in sheets.
Now we walk on the ice, with slow steps,
Attentive how we walk, for fear of falling;

If we move quickly, we slip and fall to earth,
Again walking heavily on the ice,
Until the ice breaks and dissolves;

We hear from the closed doors
Boreas and all the winds at war—
This is winter, but such as brings joy.

Particularly through the part of the bass, the winter concerto portrays a musical landscape that is frozen and desolate. A solo violin is played furiously to depict the harshness of the frigid wind. In later sections, the violins sound like teeth chattering together in the fierce Venetian cold. The second movement describes a fire, while the third depicts walking on thin ice. Then, in the final movement, there is a battle of the north and south winds.

Antonio Vivaldi dedicated *The Four Seasons* to Count Venceslaus von Morzin of Bohemia in typically dramatic fashion:

…I have decided to engrave the present volume and to submit it to the feet of Your Illustrious Grace; I beg you not to be surprised if among these few and feeble concertos, Your Illustrious Grace will find the Four Seasons, already long since under the indulgent and generous eye of Your Grace, but may you believe me that I took great pride in publishing them…

Although he never made it to France, Vivaldi's music was wildly successful in Paris. His *Four Seasons* had been performed to such adulation that the French Ambassador, Jacques-Vincent Languet, Count of Gergy, asked Vivaldi to compose a cantata, a song in praise of Paris, to be played when he made his public entry into Venice in 1726.

La Senna festeggiante is Vivaldi's most famous cantata, and one of the few that still exists. Vivaldi imitated the much more ornamental French style when he wrote this piece. French Baroque music had more embellishments than did Italian compositions, but tended to be slower in tempo. Composing the piece in their style was a gesture of goodwill, and it made Vivaldi all the more adored by the French.

Vivaldi also wrote *La Gloria*, a serenata (a dramatic vocal work to be sung outdoors), for the wedding of Louis XV to the Polish Princess Maria Leszczynska. This work, scored for chorus and orchestra, remains one of Vivaldi's most popular religious pieces.

After his short but creative stay in Rome, Vivaldi traveled the long distance to Vienna, Austria in 1728, before going to Trieste to direct performances for Holy Roman Emperor Charles VI, a music lover under whose reign opera in Vienna flourished. It had been a busy time for the emperor. He had been negotiating diplomatic treaties with Spain, Prussia, and Great Britain to ensure that, because he had no male heirs, his daughter Maria Theresa would be allowed to inherit his throne. Although very busy, the emperor found time to share thoughts about music with Vivaldi and wrote in a letter that he spoke more with Vivaldi during the composer's two-

The Austrian city of Vienna, seen here in the mid-1700s. The impressive spire of St. Stephen's cathedral extends high above the skyline. *(Courtesy of Malvisi Archive, Populonia.)*

week stay than he had with his court ministers in two years. For his time and service, the Emperor honored Vivaldi with money, a gold medal, and a knighthood. Naturally, Vivaldi returned the gesture by dedicating the twelve violin concertos of his Opus 9 to him.

Vivaldi did not travel alone. Because of his health condition, he usually needed four or five people to accompany and assist him on his journeys. The added expense of lodging, food, travel expenses, and salaries for his entourage was yet another reason Vivaldi commanded such high prices for his commissioned works.

As Vivaldi's fame and notoriety swelled he never forgot the role his father had played in his artistic development. In 1729, he invited his seventy-five year old father to join him in his travels. Giovanni took a leave of absence from the St. Mark's orchestra, where he still played violin, to go abroad with his now-famous son. Records show that Giovanni never returned to playing at St. Mark's, and historians believed, for a time, that he must have passed away at some point on the tour. In actuality, father and son lived together off and on for the next several years, and it was in their apartment that Giovanni passed away in 1736, a proud man who had lived long enough to see his son achieve great fame.

Chapter Five
Rumors

As Antonio Vivaldi became increasingly popular, curious fans wanted to know more about his private affairs. What the public did not know for certain, they made up. Over time, stories about the redheaded priest circulated widely, and since Vivaldi himself wrote very few letters to set things right, historians have had to dig through scant evidence to try to piece together an accurate picture.

Rumor had it, for instance, that Vivaldi was not just a celibate priest, but actually a eunuch (a man who has been castrated). This rumor originated when Edward Wright, a traveler through Italy, wrote that the girls at the Pietà "have a eunuch for their master, and he composes their music." Where Wright came up with that information, no one knows. A man working so closely with so many young ladies may have been discomfiting to some people, and perhaps that is why Wright decided to claim that Vivaldi lacked the ability to be sexual with them. It is possible he heard the rumor from someone else and he was merely the first person to put the idea into print. There is, however, no reason to believe the rumor was true.

The most damaging rumors had to do with a lovely young soprano that Vivaldi met in 1724 in Mantua. Anna Giraud was singing in the opera *Laodicea* by Tomaso Albinoni. She was the daughter of a French barber, but had been born in Mantua. Described as elegant and small in frame, Anna was said to have "beautiful eyes and a fascinating mouth." She was seventeen and Vivaldi was forty-eight when he decided to take her on as his protégée. He taught her some singing techniques particular to his operas and cast her as Regina Tamiri in his opera *Farnace,* which played in 1727 at the San Grisostomo Theater. Vivaldi highlighted her talent with the unique aria "The sweet and dear emotion in the breast," which also featured a Corno di Caccia (hunting horn), an instrument that until this point had only been used during hunting scenes in operas.

Abbé Antonio Conti wrote of Anna's performance in *Farnace,* "The music is by Vivaldi, it is very varied both in its sublime and tender moments; his pupil performed miracles even if her voice is not one of the most beautiful." Many critics of the time agreed that Anna had a great talent for acting but that her voice was small.

Vivaldi seemed content with both her acting and singing, because he continued to feature her in his operas for the next twenty-three years.

Vivaldi had his operas performed in multiple cities, and Anna traveled with him from venue to venue. Her sister Paolina joined the entourage as well, both to chaperone and to serve as a nurse to Vivaldi, who continued to suffer ill health.

Not only did rumors circulate that Vivaldi was having a love affair with Anna, but some people thought he was romantically involved with Anna's sister, Paolina, as well. Anyone who thought the redheaded priest was a eunuch must have been confused by the gossip. These rumors are unlikely to have been true, given his devotion to the Church. Also, if the Church had believed such rumors, there would have been an investigation and possibly dire consequences for Vivaldi.

Members of the clergy were held to very strict laws, including a vow of celibacy. Vivaldi, as a priest, was such a public figure it seems unlikely he would have risked his career and his livelihood by openly keeping one mistress, much less two.

Whether or not the rumors were true, Vivaldi's protective behavior towards Anna only intensified them. An instance of such behavior occurred soon after he first met the young woman. Anna had just made her debut in his opera and had won the favor of Alderano IV Cybo, Duke of Massa. The Duke gave her sixty zecchini as a present—no small sum considering that one gold zecchina was worth twice a silver ducat. Anna wanted to use the money to buy herself a particular harpsichord, built by the celebrated craftsman Dominco da Pesaro.

Anna asked Vivaldi to help her negotiate the purchase from Andrea Bonazza, the instrument's owner. Vivaldi arranged to have her pay thirty zecchini for the harpsichord. When Bonazza later found out that the Duke had given her sixty zecchini, he thought that all of the money had been intended for the purchase of the harpsichord and that Vivaldi had cheated him out of half the money. Bonazza took the composer and the singer to court. Vivaldi wrote a long, detailed letter to the judge and, in the end, Bonazza did not get any more money and Anna got to keep the harpsichord. That Vivaldi went to such lengths for this woman suggested to many that his

The tinny, plucked sound of the harpsichord was an important element of Baroque music.

affections for her went far beyond the pupil/tutor relationship he professed.

Another reason people believed Vivaldi and Anna
Giraud were more than colleagues was due to a mistake
made by Zuanne Zuccato, the Neapolitan Ambassador
to the Venetian government. Reporting on the theater
scene, he wrote home "...there are fine voices which are
naturally exceptional, also that of Annina from the Pietà
who is now creating a furor at all the best theaters,
namely at S. Angelo, and she has no equals..." While
Zuccato meant to compliment Anna, in doing so, he
identified her as a student from the Pietà, which she was
not.

Many years later, in 1729, the Holy Inquisition would
catch a male musician in a brothel with a young lady and
"Anna who sings at the Pietà" would be cited as a
witness. Vatican secret agents eventually discovered
that some of the women from the *Pietà* were operating
brothels and sometimes sent the girls to work in them for
brief periods. While Anna Giraud was certainly not the
same "Anna from the Pietà" cited in this case, the
confusion from Zuccato's error did not help her reputation, or Vivaldi's.

There was another rumor about Vivaldi, but this one
held far less shame. It had to do with how quickly Vivaldi
could write. Given the amount of music Vivaldi created
every month, he had to be very prolific. Since the public
was so hungry for new material, and pieces were rarely
performed at more than one festival or concert season,

The speed with which Vivaldi wrote his music can nearly be felt in this hand-written edition of one of his hugely popular violin concertos.

he learned to write both quickly and well. He could write four full operas a year without missing the deadline for the two concertos a month he owed the *Pietà*. At the same time he might be composing smaller works for whatever noble had currently hired him or for his high-paying students. Many composers wrote at phenomenal speed in the Baroque period, but Vivaldi holds the record. He once boasted to a friend that he had written his opera *Tito Manlio* in five days.

Vivaldi was extremely proud of being known for the sheer speed at which he could work. He often said he could write a complete concerto in less time than it could be copied. He told one impresario that he had written ninety-four operas over his lifetime. This is certainly not impossible, but might have been an exaggeration. Today we know of only forty-seven Vivaldi operas.

There was a trick to Vivaldi's speed, however, and few patrons of the time figured it out. With the huge library of material that he created over the years, most of it having been heard only once, he could easily lift segments from one piece and drop them into other pieces. No one was the wiser. One example is his concerto for treble recorder, RV. 442, which shows up again, with few changes, in Opus 10, a collection of flute concertos. Strains of *The Four Seasons* can be heard in his opera *Orlando Furioso*. Because of the widespread availability of recorded music, this same practice could not go on today, but back then, after a few years had gone by and a piece of music was more or less forgotten, there was little to prevent a composer from raiding his earlier scores for "new" material.

Vivaldi took special advantage of this trick when he wrote for private audiences. When Uffenbach requested music by Vivaldi and the composer appeared three days later with ten concertos, Uffenbach guessed, and rightly so, that Vivaldi did not actually write that much music in such a short period of time. The master found some pieces he had never published, cleaned them up, perhaps made a few changes, and sold them to the German visitor as new works.

Though he usually got away with it, this practice angered one impresario named Luca Casimiro degli Albizzi. "You will do as I said and said repeatedly to you," he scolded Vivaldi, "not to seek out old arias and then include them arbitrarily as you see fit."

Writing operas quickly seemed not a particular challenge for Vivaldi. He created a formula that satisfied his audiences and molded all of his compositions to it. Since most people went to the opera for entertainment, they were not looking for masterpieces. They hoped to see their favorite singers performing the latest songs, and eagerly anticipated the embellishments during the last portion of the arias, the only point in an opera where they welcomed surprises. They might even attend several performances of the same show, simply to hear the different improvisations a singer would attempt.

When Vivaldi composed for the theater, he followed a simple pattern. He drove the story forward through the conversations sung between characters, called recitatives. To keep the heavy orchestration from muddling the more important lyrics in these sections, Vivaldi would often have the recitatives accompanied quietly by a lone harpsichord. When the full orchestra began to play, it signaled the beginning of an aria. The arias were often inner monologues of the characters.

As with most other operas of the Baroque period, Vivaldi's have not stood the test of time as well as his concertos have. However, they achieved their goal of pleasing audiences in their day. The composers of the future Classical and Romantic periods would create new conventions and methods for telling stories that raised the form of opera to a higher level. Although Baroque music is ornately beautiful, today the plots come across as ridiculous and trite. The few that remain are studied

One of Venice's grand theaters, the *Teatro San Samuele*, where Vivaldi's opera, *Griselda,* was scheduled to be performed. *(Courtesy of Museo Correr, Venice.)*

for their historical value but are rarely staged.

Despite Vivaldi's reputation in Italy for being a talented composer who could write very quickly, he was himself amazed at the speed of another artist. Carlo Goldoni was a playwright who was hired to write the libretto for *Griselda*, an opera to be composed by Vivaldi and performed at the Teatro San Samuele. Anna Giraud was to sing the role of Griselda, but one aria in the opera did not suit her. Vivaldi invited Goldoni over to look at the story and try to write something that would work better. Goldoni shocked Vivaldi when he told the composer he would write the new lyrics right there in his parlor. While Vivaldi dutifully did his daily prayers, Goldoni set to work. Fifteen minutes later he completed the new lyrics. Goldoni wrote of the event:

> I took my work to him. With his breviary in his right hand and my sheet of paper in his left he began to read gently. When he had finished he threw the breviary into a corner, got up, embraced me, ran to the door and called Signora Annina. Annina arrived, with her sister Paolina. He read them the arietta, shouting: 'He did it here, he did it here on this very spot!' Again he embraced me and congratulated me, and now I had become his friend, his poet, his confident, and he never abandoned me.

Even though he was known for possessing an enormous ego regarding his work, Vivaldi demonstrated in this situation that he could still fully appreciate a fellow artist who exhibited an equal level of skill.

For many years the people of Europe entertained themselves by guessing at the nature of Vivaldi's personality and behaviors; they did not generally hold any of it against him. They cared more for the quality of his music. Gradually, however, that began to change. As he entered his fifties, Vivaldi found himself working harder than ever to stay in the favor of his patrons. For example, in the fall of 1728, he found himself in Geneva where he met Duke Carl Ludwig Friedrich. The twenty-year-old Duke played flute and wanted private music lessons from Vivaldi. Always one to oblige a wealthy nobleman,

Vivaldi took him in as a student when Friedrich arrived in Venice the following year.

Their association was unusually brief. Most of his pupils studied with him for long periods of time, so that Vivaldi could write music specifically for them and he could ready them for a public debut. This was not the case for the Duke, and Vivaldi could not understand why Friedrich abandoned his studies so abruptly. Vivaldi wrote letters to Friedrich for another year, continuing to offer his services. His overtures were not accepted, and Vivaldi considered this rejection a deliberate insult.

In his final letter to the Duke, Vivaldi wonders if he "still find[s] pleasure in playing the flute." There is a hint of desperation in the missive. It suggests that Vivaldi

Artists of all types, including composers and musicians, relied on the patronage of wealthy fans in order to continue working at their art. As Vivaldi's popularity began to diminish, he feared he would lose favor with his financial backers. *(Courtesy of Professor Denis Stevens.)*

THE PATRONAGE SYSTEM

A career as an artist was one of the very few outside of the church that allowed a young man to advance in the rather strict social hierarchy of Vivaldi's Europe. A promising young artist could usually find a patron—a wealthy person, often of the nobility—who would sponsor the artist at the outset of his career.

The most fortunate artists were taken up by patrons who gave them a place to live and money for living expenses, paid full market prices for their completed work, paid for travel the artist might undertake to learn from another person or place, and sometimes even gave the artist a title in his court. Since it was in the patron's best interests for his artist to succeed, the patron would praise his protégé's work and encourage the artist to accept commissions from the patron's friends. Once an artist became well-known and established, he would leave the patron's house to open his own studio where he would receive commissions from a variety of sources, including individuals, churches, and even villages.

An artist's success depended on how well he could please his customers. Artists were often given exact guidelines for paintings, including the precise dimensions of the picture, whether it was to be part of a set (paintings were often ordered in pairs for symmetry), and even instruction as to the content of the picture and which colors should be used. Detailed contracts specified whether an artist had to present sketches or samples of his work and time was always a factor. Artists who could work quickly benefited financially. Prices varied widely depending on the status of the artist and the work commissioned. Some artists would charge for the number of figures in the painting, some for the piece as a whole, and still others would demand a salary for larger works that would consume months or even years of their time.

really needed the employment, perhaps to quell the unease he felt at being rejected or to prevent others from learning that he had lost a valued benefactor. Once the noble class learned that he had been passed over, he stood to lose more patronage. Spending money and attention on composers and artists was a fashion statement, and Vivaldi did not want to be considered out of style.

Try as he might to avert or disguise the fact, Vivaldi's career was beginning to decline. His operas were not as popular as they had once been. His lightning-quick composing speed was now merely a novelty, and the rumors about his relationship with Anna Giraud were threatening to overwhelm his musical reputation. In addition, to Vivaldi's dismay, a much younger composer named Johann Adolph Hasse had emerged on the scene, and all of Venice was wild about him. At the age of fifty-two, Vivaldi was beginning to be seen as old-fashioned and passé.

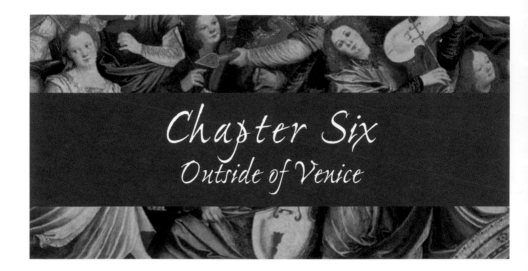

Chapter Six
Outside of Venice

Johann Adolph Hasse was German and, at thirty-one, he was twenty-one years younger than Vivaldi. He had been a tenor singer before he began composing operas of his own in 1721. For the previous four years he had studied in Naples, Italy under Domenico Scarlatti, an internationally famous harpsichord virtuoso. Hasse debuted in Venice with his opera *Artaserse,* libretto by Pietro Metastasio, at the San Giovanni Grisostomo the-ater. The cast featured a number of stars, including Hasse's wife, Faustina Bordoni. The city lavished money and gifts on the imported production. The leading con-tralto singer alone was paid five times more than Vivaldi had ever earned from an opera.

Spending all this money on an opera may have been part of the city's attempt to reinvigorate its economy. In the past, Venice had been one of the richest cities in the western world, thanks to its pivotal spot along the trade routes. But in recent years the once profitable industries of printing and glass-making were now doing better business in the Netherlands and France. Vivaldi was at least partially responsible for this because it was his work with Estienne Roger that had started the trend of sending music out of Venice to be printed. Also, ships now were much bigger and faster, making it easier for them to sail around the cape of Africa to the Atlantic coast of Western Europe. They rarely neared Venice's shores in the Adriatic

Above: Opera singer Faustina Bordoni. *Below:* Her husband, the German composer Johann Adolph Hasse. *(Courtesy of Kupferstich-Kabinett, Dresden.)*

This section of the mural that decorates the walls and ceiling of St. Mark's Chapel exemplifies typical Venetian decadence. The woman accessorizes her gown with jewels and feather boas. The glittering gold backdrop adds to the overall sense of luxury and wealth that characterized the port city for so many years.

Sea anymore. Few people in Venice earned the same income their fathers had enjoyed before them.

The Venetians were proud people, and even as their city dwindled into its final days of grandeur, they carried on as if nothing had changed. Men and women still dressed in the most ornate fashions and lived in grand houses with waterfront views. There is even a legend of one Venetian merchant who took out a second mortgage on his palatial home simply so that he could throw an extravagant party. He hoped no one would discover that his serving staff had been rented for the evening.

Music remained one of the primary reasons people

traveled to the city of canals. It made sense that if the Venetians spent money on anything, it would be on the newest and brightest opera stars and composers. A large investment in a musical production could pay off if the show was exciting enough to draw tourists. By this time, however, fifty-two-year-old Vivaldi and the singers he usually employed had been around for seventeen years. Audiences were hungry for new names and faces. Financial backers considered it too risky to put money into his shows. When they did choose to support a Vivaldi opera, they certainly did not pay him the same high rates that Hasse commanded.

Venice became enamored with Hasse. Even Vivaldi's protégée, Anna Giraud, honored the new composer by starring in his opera *Dalisa* at the San Angelo Theater. Because of this, Vivaldi knew he had to move to more fertile ground. He had heard that Antonio Denzo had taken his Italian opera troupe to Prague back in 1724, and had been so successful he had not yet returned to Venice. Vivaldi took his entourage north once again. In Prague, he remounted his favorite showpiece, *Farnace,* and two other operas during his two-year stay. He also made an impact with his sacred music.

In 1732, a new theater had opened in Verona, Italy. For the opening performance, the impresario of the theater wanted an opera by G. M. Orlandini, the maestro di cappella of Florence Cathedral who was celebrated for his dramatic music. Orlandini could not fulfill the obligation and Vivaldi was the second choice. He was not the composer that the leading male soprano, a castrato named Francesco Bilanzoni, wanted, though. Bilanzoni refused to play the role he was offered despite the large salary that accompanied it. The production was nearly cancelled. At the last minute, the impresario pulled together a cast of less adequate singers and a small

CASTRATI

In the Baroque era, particularly in the Catholic areas of Europe, women and girls were not permitted to sing in church services. In the all-male choirs, pre-pubescent boys whose voices had not yet changed sang the high parts and some of the most talented boy singers were also selected to sing in operas.

The castrato Farinelli, playing a female leading role, as drawn by the caricature artist, P. L. Ghezzi.

As hormone production increases during puberty, the male vocal chords enlarge, causing the voice to deepen. This basic fact of life presented problems for opera directors, who had to constantly replace these singers. A solution, albeit brutal, was found. Castrating a young singer before his voice deepened could preserve the boy's high voice. The combination of a young boy's vocal chords with the powerful lung capacity of a man made for a unique voice with incredible range.

A great degree of honor was involved with the rather gruesome procedure, as only the very best singers were selected to become castrati. Unfortunately, the removal of the testicles often led to a range of physical, psychological, and emotional problems. Some castrati became overweight or deeply depressed.

Though originally sanctioned by the Church, the practice was eventually condemned. Carlo Broschi Farinelli was the most celebrated castrato.

The great castrato, Farinelli, pictured here with his friend, the soprano Teresa Castellini, c. 1751. *(Detail from a painting by Jacopo Amigoni.)*

budget and managed to save the show. Critics gave it bad reviews.

Vivaldi became more desperate for money. It may have been simple greed, but more than likely he felt he deserved to make as much money for his music as other composers were making. After all, he had been around longer and had paved the way for these young upstarts. But few besides Vivaldi thought he was worth such enormous salaries any longer.

He decided to quit publishing his concertos, believing he could make more money selling them to private collectors. A 1733 letter from Edward Holdsworth to music connoisseur and patron Charles Jennens comments, "...[Vivaldi] expects a guinea for every piece. Perhaps you might deal with him if you were here to choose what you like, but I am sure I shall not venture to choose for you at that price." The letter suggests that Vivaldi was demanding too much for his work.

Money affected Vivaldi's next production in Verona as well. Count Rambaldo Rambaldi, the leading member of the Veronese Accademia Filarmonica, was in charge of the Veronese theater. When Vivaldi insisted on eight hundred ducats for his opera and another eight hundred ducats for his leading male performer, Rambaldi balked. The theater would not pay that much money, especially after Vivaldi's last Veronese opera had turned out to be such a failure.

Although his work was still respected in Verona, Vivaldi's self-glorification had started rubbing people the wrong way. Insisting on such a large sum nearly prevented the opera from being produced at all. In the end, Vivaldi must have sensed that he was losing the battle and that a little money was better than none, for he agreed to stage *L'Adelaide* for half of his initial request.

To soothe tensions, Vivaldi wrote to Rambaldi and the Filarmonica, "...nothing shall prejudice the performances, on the contrary... all shall be harmonious... so I dare to hope for the welcome of Your Illustrious Selves

Verona was among the cities to become disenchanted with Vivaldi's work later in his career. *(Painting by Bernardo Bellotto.)*

and of the whole community whose appropriation I trust that my efforts will merit." The letter may have eased the nerves of his benefactors during production of the opera, but it failed to mend things entirely. Vivaldi was not invited back to Verona.

The following year Antonio Vivaldi's contract was renewed once more at the Pietà, but this time the governors decided to limit how much time he could spend away from the orphanage. In addition to their concerns about his travels, some of the governors worried that Vivaldi's reputation had become tarnished and might reflect badly upon the girls and the school. He was fortunate to keep his steadily paying position as maestro di cappella for the next few years.

The end of his most productive years came in 1737 when Vivaldi went south to Ferrara, Italy. A good friend, the Marquis Guido Bentivoglio, operated as the middleman between Vivaldi and the Ferrara opera impresario Abbé Bollani to arrange for two of Vivaldi's operas to be staged there. Once again Vivaldi found himself in the middle of tense negotiations. He began by insisting on being paid ten more zecchini than Bollani was willing to pay for a completely new work. Ultimately, Vivaldi wound up compromising, as he had in Verona, by offering two arrangements of pre-existing operas for little more than a copyist would charge.

Vivaldi had agreed to sell Bollani his operas *L'Olimpiade,* a romantic play about the Olympic games, and *La Ginevra.* Both of the operas would need revision, so Vivaldi set to work. Once he had completely revised *La Ginevra,* Bollani changed his mind, deciding he wanted Vivaldi to create a new arrangement of *Demetrio* by Hasse instead of *La Ginevra.* Vivaldi agreed to the change of plans and started on a major reconstruction of the work so that it would be more up to date and better suit his performers.

He sent his compositions to Bentivoglio rather than directly to the impresario for fear that Bollani would get too excited and throw a fit if he disliked any of the music. Vivaldi had no interest in any of the impresario's critiques. He was halfway through his revision of *L'Olimpiade* when Bollani changed his mind again. This time he decided he wanted Vivaldi to rearrange yet another opera not his own, *Alessandro nell'Indie,* in place of *L'Olimpiade.*

Outraged, Vivaldi wrote a letter to his friend

Bentivoglio complaining about how incompetent this impresario from Ferrara was: "In many letters he torments me to send him *L'Olimpiade*. I adjust it, even ruining my original in doing so... And there—another command: he does not want *L'Olimpiade* any longer, but *L'Alessandro in Indie*."

Vivaldi insisted on more money to compensate for his inconvenience and trouble. To Bentivoglio he wrote, "Can Your Excellency imagine that this impresario merits the corrections of four operas instead of two, the redone recitatives, all the services and on top of it, those expenses? With Your Excellency's generosity, he shall have to reimburse me for all this."

After agreements were finally reached about which operas were to be staged and how much Vivaldi would be paid—but before he could pack his bags and take his troupe to Ferrara for Carnival season—a new problem arose. This time the trouble had to do not with the theater, but the Church. Cardinal Tomaso Ruffo, the head of the Catholic Church in Ferrara, believed Vivaldi's relationship with Anna Giraud was an inappropriate one for a priest to have. He also refused to believe that Vivaldi's health prohibited him from saying Mass. The cardinal barred Vivaldi from entering Ferrara.

After all his preparation for the opera season, this order from the cardinal was a terrible setback. Vivaldi had already spent a great deal of his own money for expenses toward the opera production and was contractually responsible for a great deal more. If he did not go to Ferrara and mount his operas, he stood to lose a tremendous amount of money. He wrote to Bentivoglio to complain of the cardinal's treatment and to beg that his operas be cancelled, which would at least let Vivaldi out of his contract and the additional money he was due to pay. He wrote: "It is impossible to do the opera without me, because I will not entrust such a large sum to other hands. I am, moreover, bound by the contracts; therefore, alas, I have a mountain of difficulties."

Despite Bentivoglio's influence in the small city, he could not get the operas cancelled. They went on as scheduled, without Vivaldi. Cardinal Russo had severely damaged the composer's reputation and added grist to the rumor mill. Now people began speculating about Vivaldi's friendship with Anna even more and openly wondered if he was really ill. After all, if the maestro was well enough to travel, compose, conduct, and play violin, how sick could he be? Celebrating Mass should not have been such a problem for him. A rumor began to circulate that Vivaldi had ducked out

Because of his poor health, Vivaldi needed assistance simply going into the busy town to shop. (Detail of Canaletto's "The Clockwork in the Piazzo San Marco, 1728-30.)

of Mass years before because he had a musical idea and could not wait to get back to his antechamber and put it to paper. The idea that a priest considered his music more important than his religious duties shocked many in Venice.

Vivaldi protested that being able to do his work did not mean he was well. He explained again and again that the reason his expenses were so high was because he had to maintain a staff of people to take care of him when he traveled; the dutiful Giraud sisters were among those employees. Vivaldi claimed that he never walked anywhere but always went about town in a covered coach. To make things easier, he had his employers come to his home rather than going through the tiring ordeal of getting to them. As for playing the violin, he only played for the opening performance of an opera, and then only because he was in great demand.

None of his protests seemed to help. Attendance at his operas dropped as audiences turned from him. Ironically, he was being punished for his musical ambition. Vivaldi's cravings for fame had driven him to fantastical musical heights. His compositions were the result of his desire to please audiences that now cared little for him. Vivaldi's ambition had made him a pariah.

The following year his opera *Siroe* was scheduled to be performed at the Reggio Emilia Theater in Ferrara, but the cardinal still would not allow Vivaldi or Anna Giraud into the city. This time Vivaldi was persuaded to hand control of his opera to Francesco Picchi, a theater

An opera rehearsal in the mid-1700s.

impresario he considered inept. Again, the opera was a dismal failure.

There was talk of canceling Vivaldi's second opera of the season, but he begged his friend Bentivoglio to intervene and to make sure *Farnace* was staged. This was a mistake. Without his presence, the performance spun out of control. The harpsichordist rewrote some of the recitatives without permission, and the impresario could not control the musicians, a job normally handled by the composer. Afraid of yet another failure with Vivaldi's name on it, the musicians altered his music to sound more contemporary. However, their caution only ensured that what they feared most would happen. The audiences disliked the opera, though it had always been successful when performed in other cities.

Vivaldi complained to his friend: "Excellency, I am desperate, I can not bear that such an ignoramus makes his fortune on the ruin of my poor name. I humbly beseech you not to forsake me, because I swear to Your Excellency, if my reputation is at stake I shall take action to defend my honor, for he who takes my honor from me, takes my life."

Bentivoglio found himself in a difficult spot. He wanted to help his good friend, but to do so could ruin his own reputation. In the end, he refused to involve himself any further in Vivaldi's unfortunate situation.

The disaster in Ferrara concluded in early 1739 when the bills for operas poured in. Vivaldi found himself in a great deal of debt to the performers and set designers. One painter filed a lawsuit against him, but Vivaldi countered by accusing the painter of embezzling money. In the end the "not unimportant sum" of money he claimed Vivaldi owed him would never be paid.

In spite of his lengthy problems in Ferrara, Vivaldi managed to stay busy with other projects. Vivaldi spent a portion of that time in Amsterdam, where he had been invited to celebrate the hundredth anniversary of the Schouwberg theater. He also conducted the festival program on January 7, 1738, which included an opera and a cantata. The program opened with the *Concerto Grosso à 10 Stromenti, due corni a caccia, tympano, due oboe, violino principale, due violini, alto-viola con basso* written specifically for the players in the court orchestra.

That same year, the only compositions Venice wanted from Vivaldi were two pasticcios (compositions created from pieces of earlier works), revised versions of *Armida al campo d'Egitto* and *Rosmira fedele*. Most of his work in these later years involved arranging and editing other composers' operas rather than writing his own. His final full opera, *Feraspe*, with a libretto by Francesco Silvani, was staged at the San Angelo theater in 1739. The performance was so unpopular that talk of mounting any more Vivaldi works ended. Works by more popular composers, such as young Hasse, were chosen instead.

After his bad luck in Verona, Ferrara, and Venice it seemed as if Italy was through with Antonio Vivaldi. Convinced his name still meant something elsewhere in Europe, Vivaldi, at sixty-one years old, decided to leave Italy.

Chapter Seven
Out of Fashion

1739 was the last year of Vivaldi's employment at the girls' orphanage. The board of governors resented that he had not made the Pietà orchestra his priority. Except for one performance in 1740, before the Elector Friedrich Christian of Saxony, for which the school hired Vivaldi to conduct one of his concertos, he was no longer asked to provide music. Like the rest of Venice, the governors of the Pietà now preferred newer and younger composers such as Giuseppe Tartini, a violinist from Padua who was quickly becoming famous for his string ensemble compositions. Vivaldi's close friend Charles de Brosses wrote in 1739, "To my great surprise I found that he is not so highly regarded as he deserves to be in this country, where everything follows the fashions, where his works have been heard for too long a time, and where

The female singers and string players, shown in the upper left of this painting by Francesco Guardi, are believed to be from the Pio Ospedale della Pietà.

last year's music is no longer box-office."

After thirty-six years of service to the school, all the governors offered Vivaldi was a token amount of money for a new set of concertos, a far cry from the sum they had paid him when he was at the height of his popularity. Vivaldi must have been desperate for any money at all, or he would have never accepted such meager fees. He was paid on May 12, 1740.

He left town within days of receiving the payment, for a record shows that sixteen days later authorities showed up at his house to deliver a summons for Vivaldi to detail his composing fees for the opera *Feraspe*. Some of the singers still had not been paid, and the matter was before the court. Vivaldi's statement was never provided. When the authorities arrived, his neighbors told them that Antonio Vivaldi was out of town and was not planning to return.

Anna Giraud had been singing in Vivaldi's *Catone* in Utica that April in Graz, Austria. He joined her there for a short while, but their association soon ended. Anna had her own career now, and Vivaldi could no longer support her artistically or financially. He was an old man of sixty-two by this time, plagued with illness, and Anna was a vivacious thirty-three years old. Details of their relationship's demise are not known. Anna might have abandoned Vivaldi in his last days, or he could have gracefully removed himself from her presence. Anna Giraud would die ten years later.

Alone, Vivaldi headed to Vienna. His hope was to once again find employment with Emperor Charles VI, who had so enjoyed Vivaldi's stay twelve years earlier that he had honored Vivaldi with a knighthood. Unfortunately, the Emperor died later that year, in October, from eating poisonous mushrooms. Maria Theresa and her consort Francis Stephen, another man who had been a patron of Vivaldi's music in the past, assumed power.

The new Empress did not have time for music, though. Frederick the Great of Prussia had taken advantage of this vulnerable time to attack Austria beginning the War of Austrian Succession. All of the country's resources

Frederick the Great of Prussia. His invasion of Austria in 1740 came without warning, and at a time of great vulnerability for the Austrian empire. He attacked during the transition of leadership from Holy Roman Emperor Charles VI to his daughter, Maria Theresa. *(Courtesy of Rainsville Archive.)*

went to fund the army. Vivaldi had no hope of making a living as a composer there.

Although there were plenty of other cities in Europe where he could have still made some small living, Vivaldi chose to remain in Vienna. His health had worsened, and he was running out of money. The once beloved composer was now, tragically, nearing a state of pennilessness, and could no longer afford an entourage to care for him when he traveled. Assuming that he would work until the day he died, Vivaldi continued to freely spend the little money he still had, not saving any for the day when his work ceased to be in demand.

On June 28, 1741, Vivaldi sold a number of compositions to Antonio Vinciguerra, Count of Collalto. The Count was a Venetian nobleman, but he lived primarily in Moravia. This would be the last money Vivaldi earned for his work.

Since his arrival in Vienna, Vivaldi had been living in a rented room in a large four-story house centrally located in the city, only steps away from the Kärntnertortheater, a theater that had produced nine of his operas over the past decade. The house was more than two hundred years old and owned by the widow of a man named Waller, who had worked as a craftsman, making saddles. In years to come this house would be used for rehearsals for the opera house and many of the artists who performed there would rent the rooms. Vivaldi

St. Stephen's Cathedral, Vienna, 1740. *(Courtesy of Malvisi Archive, Populonia.)*

himself may have chosen to stay there because he was hoping to stage an opera and earn some more money. But this was not to be.

Vivaldi died one month after the final sale of his music, on July 27 or 28, 1741, in Vienna. Records state that he died of "internal inflammation," a catchall phrase that offers no specifics as to the actual cause of death. The money he had earned from his last sale must have been nearly gone, for there was very little available to pay for funeral services. His legacy was exhausted to pay for the Kleingeläut, or pauper's pealing of the bells,

Composer Joseph Haydn as painted by Thomas Hardy in 1791, fifty years after he sang in the choir at Vivaldi's funeral. *(Courtesy of Victoria and Albert Museum.)*

It was months before news of Vivaldi's death in Vienna reached Venice, the city of his birth and most of his life and career. *(Courtesy of Royal Collection.)*

six pallbearers, and six choirboys from the local parish church. One of the choirboys was young Joseph Haydn, who would become a famous composer in his own right years later.

The great Antonio Vivaldi, having died a pauper, was placed in an unmarked grave in the Spitaler Gottesacker (the Hospital Cemetery), in the same ground as vast numbers of Vienna's anonymous poor. Vienna's Technical University was built over the cemetery in 1815, and Vivaldi's grave is lost.

It would be three months before his family in distant Venice learned of his death. His sisters took possession of his house and belongings to protect them from creditors. A rather frank obituary notice ran in the *Commemorali Gradenigo* in Venice:

Abbé Lord Antonio Vivaldi, incomparable virtuoso

of the violin, known as the Red Priest, much esteemed
for his compositions and concertos, who earned more
than 50,000 ducats in this life, but his disorderly
prodigality caused him to die a pauper in Vienna.

Notices of Vivaldi's death also ran in Amsterdam,
where most of his concertos had been published, and in
Paris. A year after his death, Vienna staged his *L'Oracolo
in Messenio* with this note in the playbill: "La musica è
del fù D. Antonio Vivaldi" (The music is by the late Don
Antonio Vivaldi). Other than that, no other mention or
tribute was made to the once famous music master.

Although his music had once been enormously popular, after his death Vivaldi's music was almost totally
forgotten for two hundred years. His reputation for
being overly ambitious, the unexplained relationship
with Anna Giraud, and, most of all, the change in musical
fashions, all contributed to his eclipse.

As the elaborate and formal music of the Baroque
period began to evolve and refigure itself into the more
elegant music that would be the hallmark of the Classical
period, composers like Vivaldi were forgotten. Had
Vivaldi been born ten or twenty years later he might have
been a leader in this musical revolution. As it was, his
work was old-fashioned even before his death. Many
years would pass before music lovers began looking
back to Vivaldi's time in an effort to trace the origins of
western music.

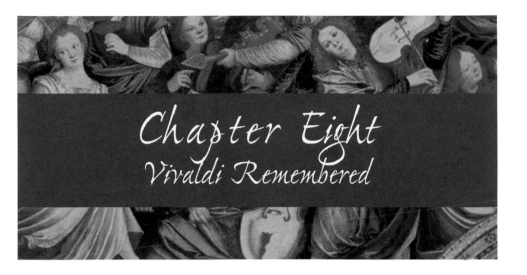

Chapter Eight
Vivaldi Remembered

In the mid-1800s, Felix Mendelssohn, a German composer of renown, began to uncover music of the past. The history of music had never been studied systematically before, and works uncovered from the Baroque and Renaissance periods thrilled Mendelssohn. The Baroque works of Johann Sebastian Bach particularly intrigued him. Then, Mendelssohn, and other scholars of Bach's music, discovered Vivaldi's name on a small handful of Bach's works: the six concertos Bach had arranged from *L'Estro Armonico*. They wondered who this Antonio Vivaldi was and what influence he had on Bach's work. A limited search was done but little was unearthed. It was decided that Vivaldi must not have been a very important composer of the Baroque Era. They could not find very many of his compositions, and the few Vivaldi concertos that Bach had toyed with were considered to be mere exercises for the harpsichord and organ.

The fact that very little of Vivaldi's work surfaced during the search was not the fault of the scholars. Their search was thorough, but his work was too deeply buried to be easily uncovered. Vivaldi's music was nearly lost to time.

Early in the twentieth century, Alberto Gentili, a professor of musicology in Turin, became interested in Vivaldi. He decided to search for the lost Vivaldi manuscripts. He spent over two decades following every lead, but he could not find a single page of music. All of the leads led him down false paths.

There was one intriguing story Gentili could not resist pursuing. He learned that in the eighteenth century the ruling court of Turin had its own orchestra. This

A scene from a spectacular ballet production in Turin from the 1600s. Turin would be an important city to the rediscovery of Vivaldi's music in the twentieth century. (Courtesy of Robert Halding Picture Library.)

group of musicians was founded on the style of violinist Giovanni Battist Somis, who had been prominent during Vivaldi's lifetime. The court orchestra had a huge library of music from the first half of the eighteenth century.

In 1796, Napoleon Bonaparte, the French conqueror, invaded Italy. The Turin court and orchestra fled to the nearby island of Sardinia in fear for their lives. The music library had to be left behind, carefully hidden so that it would not be destroyed. It was so well hidden, however, that when the war ended no one could find it again.

Oral tradition held that the library had been hidden in a monastery in Piedmont. Gentili searched and searched, but he could not find this elusive music library. Then one autumn day in 1926, to his amazement, the Vivaldi collection came to him.

A group of Benedictine monks needed to make repairs to their monastery, and they needed to raise money to do so. They were in possession of a large number of musical manuscripts and old prints that had been left to them by a prominent family. They brought the collection to Gentili at the Turin National Library to have it evaluated, hoping to sell if the manuscripts were worth anything. Buried within this mound of antique paperwork, Gentili found fourteen volumes of compositions by Antonio Vivaldi.

Marchese Marcello Durazzo, a Genoan who had been appointed Austrian Ambassador to Venice in 1765 by

Empress Maria Theresa with her family, in 1760. During her reign, music received a great deal of support.

Empress Maria Theresa, had gathered the Vivaldi music. Durazzo had been a supporter of the arts and a collector of music. After his death, Durazzo's heirs had donated the collection to the monks.

The Turin National Library could not afford to purchase the collection, so Gentili sought a patron. He had to do it secretly, for he knew that if word got out other wealthy collectors would snatch it up before the library could stake its claim. Roberto Foà, a Turin banker, agreed to fund the purchase. He bought the collection from the monks on February 15, 1927 and dedicated it to his son Mauro, who had died as a young boy.

At last Gentili had the works he had been longing to study all these years. He went to work, poring over the pages of music. To his great surprise he discovered that although he had close to three hundred concertos, eight sonatas, fourteen complete operas, five volumes of sacred works, and two volumes of secular vocal works, the numbering of the pieces showed that he had only *half* of Vivaldi's material.

Gentili concluded that Durazzo must have split the collection between his heirs. He went on another quest to find the rest of the music, but this search proved even more difficult. Once the news got out that this giant collection of Vivaldi's music had been found, avid collectors ransacked most of the monasteries in northern Italy. Instead of going that route himself, Gentili looked for a surviving member of the Durazzo family.

The last descendent, Marchese Giuseppe Maria Durazzo, was a difficult old man who did, in fact, possess the second half of the music collection. It was unorganized and gathering dust, but he had no interest in selling it. Certain he would be cheated, Durazzo negotiated only through his priest. He was finally convinced to sell in 1930.

Another patron was found to pay for this half of the collection. Coincidentally, this second patron, textile manufacturer Filippo Giordano, also had a deceased son to whom he wished to dedicate the collection. The full collection of Vivaldi's compositions is today housed in the Turin National Library and titled *Collezion Mauro Foa e Renzo Giordano,* in honor of the two lost sons. Portraits of the boys illustrate the catalogued volumes.

Now a new problem arose. When Durazzo had at last agreed to sell his half of the music he did so only on the condition that none of it ever be published or performed. This restriction was a great hindrance. The Turin Library pressed the matter in court. After nine years of civil trials the condition of the sale was overturned.

By 1939, the entire Vivaldi collection had finally been catalogued. Miss Olga Rudge, secretary of the Music Academy of Sienna, published the catalog and arranged a special honorary "Vivaldi Week" in Sienna, Italy to celebrate. At last, music from the entire Turin collection of Vivaldi's music was performed.

The Sienna celebration sparked a fascination with Vivaldi's music. Scholars began to study his works. After World War II, three orchestras dedicated themselves solely to playing Vivaldi's music. The music continued to grow in popularity throughout the second half of the century. *The Four Seasons* alone has been recorded more than one hundred times and has graced the soundtracks of many contemporary films, including *The Four Seasons*, *Shine,* and *Kramer Vs. Kramer*.

He may have been forgotten by the generation that came after him and dismissed by the Bach enthusiasts of the 1800s, but it is now clear that Antonio Vivaldi was a prominent master of music. Two hundred years of dust and neglect have not diminished the power and beauty of Vivaldi's illuminating works. His life was a roller coaster ride from the bottom to the top and back again, but the consistency of his work is remarkable. His strengths as a composer have proved to be his ultimate legacy.

Timeline

1678   Antonio Vivaldi is born on March 4, in Venice, Italy.

1689   joins the St. Mark's Cathedral orchestra and begins playing concerts with his father.

1693   begins studying for the priesthood.

1703   ordained as a priest; takes the post of violin teacher at the Pio Ospedale della Pietà.

1707   dedicates his twelve sonatas (Opus 2) for violin and harpsichord to King Frederick IV of Denmark and Norway.

1710   plays violin for Handel's *Agrippina*.

1711   publishes his *L'Estro Armonico* (Opus 3); is promoted to head composer at the Pietà.

1713   first opera, *Ottone in Villa,* opens in Venice.

1714   *Orlando finto Pazzo,* premieres.

1715   composes *Nerone fatto Cesare;* composes two oratorios, including *Juditha*.

1718   performs *Armida al camp d'Egitto* in Mantua.

1723   performs *Ercole sul Termodonte* in Rome.

1724   meets Anna Giraud.

1725   composes *The Four Seasons.*

1727- his operas *Farnace, Orlando,* and *Rosilena ed Oronta*
1728   are produced in Venice, with Anna Giraud starring.

1728   Vivaldi's father dies.

1730   Johann Adolph Hasse premieres his first opera in Venice, signaling the beginning of Vivaldi's declining popularity.

1733   Vivaldi stages *L'Adelaide* in Verona.

1739   Vivaldi's final opera, *Feraspe,* is staged in Venice; leaves the Pietà.

1740   moves to Vienna; in July, dies there.

Glossary of Musical Terms

accompaniment The music which is played beneath a solo, usually on a keyboard instrument or by an orchestra.

aria A solo song in an opera used to display both the emotion of a character and the vocal abilities of the singer.

arrangement The adaptation of a piece of music for a different combination of instruments than it was originally composed for, or for some other use for which it was not originally written.

Baroque era A period in history that dates roughly from 1600 to 1750. The most famous composers from this era are Bach, Vivaldi, and Handel.

benefactor An individual who funds an artist.

cadenza An extended solo within a piece of music. Sometimes written out by the composer, often improvised, or made up on the spot, by the performer.

cantata A religious play without scenery or staging that is sung by a choir.

castrato A male singer whose high voice was retained by castration.

cellist One who plays the cello.

composer One who writes music.

composition In Vivaldi's time, a structured piece of music written for performance by instrumental or vocal groups.

concertino (1) A small concerto. (2) The soloist group in the seventeenth and eighteenth century concerto grosso. (3) A less formally structured work than a concerto, for one or more solo instruments with orchestra.

concerto Originally, the term to describe any composition for voice and instruments during the Baroque era, now it refers more specifically to a composition that features a particular instrument with an orchestra as accompaniment.

conductor The director of a musical ensemble.

contralto The highest male voice or lowest female voice in an opera.

counterpoint A melody composed to be combined with another melody.

diva Literally, "divine." A term used to describe female opera singers.

duet A piece for two singers or other musicians.

ensemble A group of musicians playing together.

harpsichord An instrument similar to the piano, but hammers pluck rather than strike the strings. A popular instrument in Baroque music, it is the predecessor of the piano.

impresario Much like a producer on Broadway or in Hollywood, this is the person who raises the money for a performance.

librettist One who writes the words and story in an opera.

libretto Italian for *little book,* refers to the text of an opera.

lute A plucked guitar-like instrument made of wood.

madrigal A song for five or six voices, usually without accompaniment, popular in the sixteenth century.

maestro Literally, "master" in Italian. A term generally applied to the conductor of an orchestra.

Mass The central service of the Roman Catholic Church.

motets Compositions for multiple voices without accompaniment. Popular in the Middle Ages, motets could be secular or sacred, sung in Latin or French. During the Renaissance, motets became more refined in their polyphony, and sacred in subject.

movements The sections of a larger piece, usually with a particular speed or character attached to them.

opera Originating in seventeenth century Italy, a story set to music, usually entirely sung. Music, drama, scenery, costumes, dance, and other theatrical elements combine to make the art form complete.

opus Literally, "work."

oratorios Usually Biblical stories set to music, like an opera but without the staging.

orchestra A large group of instrumentalists divided into wind, brass, percussion, and string sections. The specific combination of instruments comprising an orchestra has evolved over time. In Vivaldi's day the term was used more generally, to refer to a group of instrumentalists playing together.

pasticcio A composition made up of passages taken from numerous other sources by various composers.

recitatives The conversation sections used to further the plot in an opera.

repertoire The list of pieces a certain group or soloist knows how to play.

royalties The fees collected by the artist for the sale and performance of his work.

sacred From or having to do with the church.

secular Not connected to religion.

serenata A dramatic cantata. The name is like that of a *serenade* (which is an outdoor piece) because it also took place outside, though usually at night.

solo A piece of music that is played or sung by a single performer.

sonata A composition for a solo or accompanied instrument, usually in three or four movements of varying tempo.

soprano The highest voice in a choir.

syncopation The deliberate shifting of the accent from the main beat to a weak beat or an off-beat, resulting in an unexpected change in the meter or pulse of a piece of music.

Vespers A religious service that takes place at dusk, performed by voices and sometimes accompanied by instrumentation.

virtuoso An expert performer on a particular instrument.

Sources

CHAPTER ONE: Voice of the Baroque

p. 26, "…it is hardly possible…" H.C. Robbins Landon, *Vivaldi: Voice of the Baroque.* (New York: Thames and Hudson, 1993), 50.

CHAPTER TWO: Music and the Priesthood

p. 33, "May the Lord god strike…" Denis Stevens, "Orphans and Musicians in Venice" *History Today* (http://www.findarticles.com/cf_0/m1373/5_50/62087849/p1/article.jhtml), 2.

p. 36, "Scarcely one was without…" Landon, *Vivaldi,* 30-31.

p. 37, "Enviable is the fate…" Ibid., 32.

p. 38, "I have not now said mass…" Walter Koldneder, *Antonio Vivaldi: His Life and Work* (Berkeley and Los Angeles, University of California Press, 1970), 11-12.

p. 39, "Since the sustained efforts…" Landon, *Vivaldi,* 26.

p. 44, "Realizing the necessity…" Ibid., 36.

p. 45, "Two new Mass and Vespers…" Ibid., 36.

CHAPTER THREE: Operas and Concertos

p. 50, "I must… confess…" Landon, *Vivaldi,* 46-47.

CHAPTER FOUR: The Music Business

p. 70, "Let this small tribute…" Landon, *Vivaldi,* 47.

p. 70, "The opus may gain…" Ibid., 47.

p. 71, "[He] became my intimate friend…" Ibid., 162.

p. 73, "I was at Mantua…" Kolneder, *Antonio Vivaldi,* 15.

p. 74, "…with the aforementioned Vivaldi…" Ibid., 16.

p. 82, "…I have decided to engrave…" Landon, *Vivaldi,* 67.

CHAPTER FIVE: Rumors

p. 86, "have a eunuch for their master…" Kolneder, *Antonio Vivaldi,* 16.

p. 87, "beautiful eyes…" Michael Sartoris, "Antonio Vivaldi." *Baroque Composers and Musicians* (http://www.baroque music.org/bqxvivaldi.html).

p. 87, "The music is by Vivaldi…" Landon, *Vivaldi,* 95.

p. 90, "there are fine voices…" Ibid., 97.

p. 90, "Anna who sings…" Ibid., 98.

p. 92, "You will do as I said…" Donald Levi, "Antonio Vivaldi: 1678-1741." *Music for the Mind* (http://members.tripod.com/~donlevi/vivaldi.html), 4.

p. 95, "I took my work to him…" Landon, *Vivaldi,* 124.

p. 96, "still find[s] pleasure…" Ibid., 114.

CHAPTER SIX: Outside of Venice

p. 105, "…[Vivaldi] expects a guinea…" Landon, *Vivaldi,* 117.

p. 105, "…nothing shall prejudice the performances…" Ibid., 121.

p. 108, "In many letters…" Ibid., 135.

p. 108, "Can Your Excellency imagine…" Ibid., 136.

p. 109, "It is impossible to do the opera…" Ibid., 148.

p. 112, "Excellency, I am desperate…" Ibid., 153.

p. 112, "not unimportant sum" Ibid., 159.

CHAPTER SEVEN: Out of Fashion

p. 114, "To my great surprise…," Kolneder, *Antonio Vivaldi,* 20.

p. 119, "internal inflammation" Ibid., 22.

p. 121, "Abbé Lord Antonio Vivaldi..." Landon, *Vivaldi*, 166.

Bibliography

Baker, Theodore. *Baker's Biographical Dictionary of Musicians – 8ᵗʰ Edition,* revised by Nicolas Slonimsky. New York: Schirmer Books, 1992.

Carlin, Richard. *European Classical Music 1600-1825.* New York and Oxford: Facts on File Publishing, 1988.

Catucci, Stefano. *Bach and Baroque Music.* New York: Barron's Educational Series, Inc., 1998.

Chubb, Thomas Caldecott. *The Venetians: Merchant Princes.* New York: The Viking Press, 1968.

Collison-Morley, Lacy. *Italy After the Renaissance: Decadence and Display in the Seventeenth Century.* New York: Henry Holt and Company, c.1930.

Crow, John A. *Italy: A Journey Through Time.* New York: Harper & Row Publishers, 1965.

Geringer, Karl. *Musical Instruments: Their History from the Stone Age to the Present Day.* London: George Allen & Unwin Ltd., 1965.

Grout, Donal Jay. *A History of Western Music, Third Edition.* New York: W. W. Norton & Company, Inc., 1980.

Heller, Karl. *Antonio Vivaldi: The Red Priest of Venice.* Portland, Oregon: Amadeus Press, 1991.

Koldneder, Walter. *Antonio Vivaldi: His Life and Work*. Berkeley and Los Angeles: University of California Press, 1970.

Krull, Kathleen. *Lives of the Musicians: Good Times, Bad Times (And What the Neighbors Thought)*. New York: Harcourt Brace Jovanovich Publishers, 1993.

Landon, H. C. Robbins. *Vivaldi: Voice of the Baroque*. New York: Thames and Hudson, 1993.

Moore, Douglas. *From Madrigal to Modern Music: A Guide to Musical Studies*. New York: W. W. Norton & Company, Inc., 1942.

Palisca, Claude V. *Baroque Music*. New Jersey: Prentice-Hall, Inc., 1968.

Sadie, Stanley. *The New Grove Dictionary of Music and Musicians*. Washington, D.C.: Macmillan Publishers Limited, 1980.

Sadie, Stanley, ed. *Grove Dictionary of Music & Musicians*. London, England: Macmillian, 1980.

Smith, D. Mack, *A Short History of the Italian People*. New York. Pitman Publishing Corporation. 1956.

Talbot, Michael. *Master Musicians Series: Vivaldi*. Oxford, England: Oxford University Press, 1978.

Wechsberg, Joseph. *The Pantheon Story of Music for Young People*. New York: Pantheon Books, 1968.

Web sites

About Classical Music (composer biographies, musical eras detailed, classical music glossary)
http://www.wgms.com/index.php?nid=123

Baroque Composers and Musicians
http://www.baroquemusic.org

La Couterière Parisienne (History of Costume and Fashion)
http://www.marquise.de/en

Heart's Ease: Conservatory
http://www.hearts-ease.org

Humanities Web
http://www.humanitiesweb.org

Index